The Monster
Within

The Monster Within

Overcoming Eating Disorders

Cynthia Rowland McClure

with
Paul Meier
Frank Minirth
Luis Gutierrez
Michael Moore
Richard Flournoy

© 1984 by Cynthia Rowland McClure

Published by Fleming H. Revell
a division of Baker Book House Company
P.O. Box 6287, Grand Rapids, MI 49516-6287

Spire edition published 1998

Printed in the United States of America

ISBN 0-8007-8652-1

To

Jan Sharp, because you followed your feelings. You gave me the first glimmer of hope of freedom and a new life.

Michael Moore, for pushing my buttons. Without your gift I would never have found out what the monster was or why it wanted to destroy me. Thank you eternally for being pushy, cruel, cold, yet loving me tenderly the whole three months. You saved my life!

Dr. Luis Gutierrez, for your kindness, your wisdom, your words of hope and love.

John, Jeanie, Brian, Chris, Tam, Mary, Bob, Norma, Michael, and all the other patients who, like me, wanted to die, but more importantly, wanted to fight for their lives.

Mom and Dad, for the faith in God you instilled in me, for loving me when I couldn't reach out to you, for supporting me throughout my fight to overcome the monster.

Finally, my book is dedicated to my God, for now I know you never left me. You, God, opened my blind eyes, my deaf ears. You filled up my life and helped me conquer the monster, and now you live within me.

Contents

Treating Bulimia

Foreword

This is the true story of Cynthia Rowland, a former television news reporter, who for many years had her secret personal "monster," bulimia. When Cynthia checked into the Minirth-Meier Clinic in Dallas, a Christian psychiatric center, she found an expert team of therapists who helped her battle and overcome the monster.

Cynthia was obsessed with food, forced vomiting, and laxatives. None of her family, friends, or TV fans knew she was eating up to 20,000 calories a day without gaining weight. When we admitted her to the psychiatric ward of a large general hospital, she was near death due to an electrolyte imbalance. Her emotional and spiritual depression and suicidal urges had also driven her close to dying. But she obtained victory through the power of Christ and through intensive Christian psychotherapy

Early in my residency training in psychiatry the attending professor told me and the other residents that the prevalence of different psychiatric disorders changes over the years. At that time we were attending a young woman who was blind because of what was known as "conversion hysteria." The professor said that blindness of that type had been common in years past, but was becoming much less common.

I also recall seeing in those early years of residency what was thought to be a rather rare disorder, anorexia nervosa. I can still remember my pain on hearing that one of our patients later died of it. It now appears that the eating disorders, anorexia nervosa and its related but seemingly opposite disorder, bulimia, are on the increase; at least, they are gaining increasing visibility and positive diagnosis. Every day more and more bulimic and anorexic patients are coming to our clinic. Scores of the bulimic young women have virtually the same story:

"I have had this problem for years but have not dared to tell anyone. I repeatedly binge eat and then throw up. I take at least a dozen laxatives every day. I want to stop, but I can't. I want help. Please help me!"

One day about a year ago it was my turn to make medical rounds at Richardson Medical Center. I was going to the hospital only about two or three times a month. My colleagues were in charge, and I had listened often as they told with great excitement about the eating disorder patients they were working with and the results they were having.

In the unit I visited were several people from out of state. One, Cynthia Rowland, caught my attention. She was obviously a well-motivated and intelligent young woman. She was accepted by people who knew her, but didn't feel accepted. She was smart, but didn't feel smart. She exuded confidence, but didn't feel confident. There was a radiance about her personality, but she didn't feel radiant. She was open at our first meeting, but deep within she was frightened and withdrawn. I watched with interest as she worked on her problems and became well. I was impressed as I saw her helping other young women with the same problem.

This book, then, is about Cynthia's problems and progress toward recovery, and about her love, openness, and willingness to help others. I pray God will use it to help thousands more who suffer from the same problem, and that they and others will learn to know Jesus Christ, who solves problems not only here on earth, but for an eternity.

Frank B. Minirth, M.D.

Cynthia's Story

These are my thoughts, letters, and stories about the monster that had been locked up within me for twenty-four years.

It is not only an account of my battle to overcome bulimia, but also about the people who made me understand my multiple underlying problems. In fact, it is about people who had their own monsters to conquer, and who with their love, tears, and words helped me through my death wish, my emptiness, and grieving to become truly alive for the first time in my life.

We were all fighting our own monsters: bulimia, obesity, anorexia, alcoholism, drug addiction, insomnia, depression, loneliness. We struggled to overcome our desires to die, because we desperately wanted to feel, to be full of peace and love, to be truly alive.

All the words are true. The names of the people have been changed to protect their identities.

The Monster

It lies deep inside me.

Its sole purpose is to destroy me
                     to snatch me
                        to engulf me
  when I am empty, sad, lonely, desperate, angry or
    weak.

It lives to destroy me, even when my soul feels happy
  or has just a glimmer of peace or hope.

The monster knows at exactly which moment to at-
    tack me.
It knows if I lock it up in a room inside my soul,
  I will soon release it.
The monster laughs because it knows my weakness;
  it lives to control me.
It stays within me to make sure I will perish.

The monster lives for only that purpose.

1

Is Today the Day?

Oh, please, dear Lord, let today be my last. My heart, soul, and mind know that I'm not like anyone else. I can't accept myself, it's so hard to change, to love myself, to accept my worth. It's easier to punish myself and give up. Why? Why can't I take care of myself for my own happiness? I keep thinking that someone will come into my life and make this monster, this self-hatred, go away. But I'm only fooling myself.

Every night the past ten years had been like all the others. After I had consumed perhaps six candy bars, two pizzas, a gallon of ice cream, and more candy, and had taken sixty pink pills, I came home and tried to cry. The tears would not fall; yet, my heart and soul were crying. I would pray to God to please help me realize he was all that mattered to me.

But I felt so alone. I lived only to destroy myself.

One Friday afternoon about 2 o'clock, I sat down to write my lead story for the 6 o'clock news. But the monster inside me said, "Go ahead, Cynthia, do it!" I ran to the candy machine and choked down twelve candy bars.

Then I panicked. "It's in your stomach, Cynthia. Get it out, quick, before it turns to fat." I went to the rest room, made sure no one was there, stuck my finger down my throat and threw up. Back at my desk I was sick. Still, I popped twenty laxatives into my mouth. No one, of course, was watching. I then wrote my story—a good one.

Why had I eaten twelve candy bars? Why, why, why did I do it? It was the question I kept asking, the question that had no answer. But I was helpless to stop.

At 5 o'clock I drove to a convenience store where I bought twenty dollars' worth of groceries: candy, popcorn, yogurt, peanuts, dough-nuts. I hoped no one recognized me, but the clerk looked at me and said, "Having a party?"

"The guys at the TV station are hungry," I lied.

I rushed to my car where I hurriedly opened the wrappers of all those sweet delights that I hoped would satisfy my empty soul.

I stopped at a cafeteria, where anything I wanted was waiting for the monster to consume. "Let's see. Lots of salads; maybe five. Good roughage. It will go through my stomach quickly tonight. Oh, the desserts look good." Suddenly my stomach hurt. The convenience store food was affecting me. But the pies looked good. I grabbed two pieces of chocolate pie and hoped nobody noticed. Nonchalantly I went to a corner table where no one would see me consuming all the food and popping my pink pills. Then, as I left to pay my bill, I bought three candy bars. "Something for the sweet tooth," I told the cashier.

I ran to the bathroom and threw up.

As I drove back to work, I noticed a new chicken restaurant, a drive-through. "Oh, go ahead, Cynthia," the monster whispered, "and eat, eat, eat. Kill yourself." I ordered three pieces of fried chicken, rice, and rolls.

It was time to get back to work and I gobbled the chicken dinner. As I entered the newsroom, nausea struck. I went to the bathroom to lie down, and wondered, "Oh, God, why? Why? Please, God, tomor-row. Is tomorrow the day I end this agony?"

The following night the monster struck my soul again, telling me for maybe the millionth time, "Destroy yourself, Cynthia!" I was desperate for it to be the last day of my life. My spirit could no longer live in that darkness, that secret agony of eating, of forcing food down my throat trying to feed my empty, hollow soul, of filling my stomach until it felt as though it would burst, of my back aching, and the pink pills going down. "Go ahead, destroy yourself, kill yourself. You are worthless," the monster told me.

How much money had I spent that day? Fifty dollars? What had I eaten? Doughnuts, ice cream by the gallon, pizza, sandwiches, candy and more candy? Then were there fifty pills, sixty pills, eighty pink pills that slid down my throat into my stomach?

My stomach seemed to be up to my throat. Had I gone to three different stores and three different restaurants? Pizza, a Chinese smorgasbord—take home, of course—pills, more pills, then a finger down my throat. My abdomen looked eight months pregnant, my face was swollen from all the sugar, salt, and pills. Would my bowels work? Were eighty pills enough?

I looked at the clock. It was only 6 o'clock in the evening.

Dear God, this will be the last night I do this, the last. I will destroy the monster. This living agony will end. My back aches, and my poor stomach. All that junk, the garbage, the pills. I can taste the chemicals. No, no! Please let this be a nightmare. I will wake up and this will all be a dream. Please, dear God, where are you?

The sun was shining when I woke up Sunday morning, sick, nauseated, barely able to move. My stomach was flat and I no longer looked eight months pregnant. The night before had been no dream, but a living nightmare. Suicide was the only answer.

Twelve years this has gone on, God. Today is the end! If this is my life, I won't live it. If you won't kill me, God, then I must do it myself.

At 11 o'clock church was going on and I was sure no one would miss me. After all, I had alienated myself from anyone who had ever reached out to me. Now, no one called.

Thoughts of how I would kill myself entered my mind. Visions of my brain splattered across the wall engulfed me. I thought, "The stench will be bad by the time someone finds me."

How could I get the gun? My next-door neighbors had one or two. They were protective of me. I could ask them if I might borrow one; there had been strange sounds outside my home, and if I were burglarized, how would I protect myself? My neighbor would understand. "Only for a week," I would say, "until I can afford to buy my own."

I dialed their number, but there was no answer. I waited. Tears welled up in my soul, yet I could not cry.

My soul is so numb. God, where are you? Why do you hate me, God? Why?

I lay down on the couch contemplating, envisioning my death and peace at last. Death would destroy the monster. I hated my body, my nothingness. My face was bloated, my stomach stretched. Even if I fasted for a year, I would never be skinny.

"You are nothing," the monster said. "Kill yourself, Cynthia. After all, you've been dead for so long anyway. Get the gun. Blow your brains out. You are worthless."

"Okay, okay, I will, monster. My neighbors will be home soon. Oh, please hurry. I must kill this monster."

The phone rang suddenly. Who could it be? "Please, stay away from me."

"Hello, Cynthia. This is Joan. A woman talked at church this morning. She said she almost died from bulimia, but a Christian clinic in Texas saved her. Please call her."

"Joan, I am dying."

"I know, Cynthia. Call her. Here is her number."

Why should I call her? Fifteen doctors didn't know what bulimia was. They wouldn't help me. Why should I try, take another chance? No, I wouldn't do it! A psychiatric ward? No way. Bob Rowland's daughter was supposed to work out her own problems. Besides, I didn't have the money.

But, could I do something for myself? Was it just possible I might overcome the bulimia? Maybe I shouldn't kill myself that day.

An hour passed and the monster attacked again. I ran to the store and spent $50 for groceries and pink pills. Then I made the phone call to the stranger.

"Jan," I said as tears came, "you don't know me, but I have bulimia. I want to kill myself."

"Please, what is your name?"

"My name is Cynthia Rowland."

"Cynthia Rowland, the news reporter? I have seen you on TV. Please listen to me." Her voice was shaky. "I know the agony you are going through. But, believe me, there is hope!"

"I want to kill myself, Jan. I can't go on with this monster."

"Call the Minirth-Meier Clinic in Dallas. Ask for Dr. Luis Gutierrez. Ask specifically for Mike Moore to be your therapist. He will save your life. And please, come over to see me."

I was shaking when I hung up. *Life or death, life or death, Cynthia. You have only two choices.* I dialed the number in Dallas.

The secretary had a doctor call me. He said the hospital was full and it would take a week before I could get a room. His office would call me when a bed in the psychiatric unit became available and my name came up on their waiting list.

"Oh, please," I said to myself. "Please, hurry. I can't hold on much longer."

2

One Last Chance—
Behind Locked Doors

On Monday I went to work, dead inside, a facade outside, seeming to barely hold on to my life. People in the newsroom didn't know I was planning my death. They would hate me if they knew about my monster.

But didn't they hate me already? Three weeks before, the producer had told me there were complaints about me. That cut deeply. I loved the photographers, reporters, and anchors. But it was true that lately my ability to communicate, to write, had deteriorated. The producers were down on me, and the photographers didn't talk to me. Or was it that I didn't talk to them?

"Gary, I need to talk to you," I said as I entered his office. Gary was the boss whom I admired and who always cared about me. "I have an addiction, and if I don't get help I will die." He looked at me, shocked. I was his attractive, aggressive reporter who wasn't afraid to get her feet wet, the bright, ambitious young reporter whom he had discovered at the New York Democratic Convention and offered a job. And now I was telling him I was dying.

After I explained my problem and need to go to the hospital, Gary told me to go. "I'm proud of you, Cynthia," he said. "You're young; you can overcome this. We'll be waiting for you. Do you want me to tell anyone?"

"No, please."

That week, waiting for the hospital call, was terrible. I spent money on food and pills, binging, purging, getting violently sick. I panicked often.

One night I went to Jan's house. She was lovely, with a quiet personality. The minute she saw me she embraced me. I cried. She sensed my death wish, and told me about the hospital. "You'll be behind locked doors. It is hard, but the people there care. They will help you."

I looked at her with a blind hope, hardly believing her. Yet, after she told me how she'd eat one candy bar, then take 100 pink pills, and once nearly died in the hospital, she assured me there was hope and urged me to go to Dallas.

Finally, after more binging, purging, and fasting, I called Mike Moore. "Mike, my name is Cynthia Rowland. I have bulimia. Please, I need to get to the hospital. I am getting desperate."

Coolly he said, "What do you mean, desperate?"

"I want to kill myself, but I don't want to. Please, please get me a room."

The next day the call came from the Richardson Medical Center. Frantically I threw clothes into a suitcase and went to the TV station. As I walked through the door, the newsroom was bustling. There had been a bad car wreck. The reporters' names were on the assignment wall, but mine wasn't there. I was dying and no one knew nor cared. The artist, Lauri, and I looked at each other. "Good-bye, Lauri," I said.

"Good-bye, Cynthia." I guess she thought I was going to lunch. I walked out of the newsroom and, glancing back, wondered if I would live to walk through those doors again. Would I ever be a whole person?

As I drove to the hospital, six hours away, the monster was saying, "Cynthia, you will have to back out. You don't really want to do this. Go ahead, destroy yourself." I didn't have much money, but I stopped and bought an enormous meal and ordered french fries, even though I hate them. I spent all my money on food, so had none left to buy laxatives. However, I happened to have twelve pills in my purse.

It was midnight by the time I drove into Dallas. In the hospital's parking lot, I swallowed the pills with a leftover can of pop. I looked at the hospital and felt nothing. The only thoughts I had were, "This is it, Cynthia. Either you learn to live or you will die."

The admissions lady took all my information. She told me that I had to stay in the psychiatric ward for ten days, but after that, I could leave. The maximum stay is usually sixty days. She looked at me and said, "But heaven forbid you'll have to stay that long."

I thought, "Lady, if it takes a year to destroy the monster, I will stay."

A nurse came to get me. I wanted to scream, "No, no!" I wanted to cry, but couldn't. The nurse was kind. The genuine kindness, the unfamiliar surroundings, and the strangers all made my pain and loneliness run deep. We got on the elevator and proceeded to two locked doors. She pressed a button and the doors opened automatically. We walked in. I looked back and the doors closed behind us, locking, so the monster and I couldn't escape.

By the time I unpacked and had been given a physical examination, it was 2 A.M. when I entered my room. I undressed in the dark, but could see the figure of a girl across the room, lying on her back with one knee up. In the darkness her silhouette was like one of a skeleton. I knew she was starving herself.

As I crawled into bed, the tears came. Grief, loneliness, and my ugliness overwhelmed my soul.

Oh, dear God, please be here with me. When did it begin, this emptiness, sorrow, pain? And when will it end? I feel as though I am dying physically tonight, yet I know my soul has been dead a long time. Please, God, let this be the answer to all my pain and emptiness. My cup has no drops to offer anyone. I hurt so badly, and I know tomorrow it won't get any better. Help me, God, to accept this suffering. Please help these people to heal me. I can't take this any longer.

My dreams were filled with food, gorging, and purging. When the sun came through the window, I wondered where I was. Then it hit me: I was behind locked doors.

The little skeleton silhouette got out of bed. "Hi! My name is Elizabeth. Did you come in late last night? I never heard you."

"It was after midnight."

"You're scared, aren't you?"

Tears dimmed my vision of Elizabeth. "Yes, I am."

"I know. I was too. I'm fourteen and I've never been away from home. But my anorexia was getting me down and my parents made me come. Don't worry, there aren't any crazy people here. And I promise you, you'll get used to this place."

"Will I?" I wondered. "Does it matter if I get used to it?"

Elizabeth was like an angel to me, sweet and loving. She talked about how she hurt, about missing her friends. She talked of her private school and having been close to her classmates. She touched off memories of my little school in Portland where I grew up.

Elizabeth and I looked at each other, amazed at our discoveries of similar experiences. "God," I said, "must want us together, huh, Elizabeth?"

"Yes, he must." I walked into the bathroom. Looking at the toilet, I wondered if I would ever use it to induce vomiting, and then I realized that the twelve pink pills of the night before hadn't worked. The reflection of my face in the aluminum mirror pained me—eyes swollen and skin a yellowish tint. I was so ugly. What had I done to myself? Was I ruined forever? Tears came; the monster laughed.

My first morning in the hospital, I walked into the large day room, and faces—some blank, some sad—stared at me. The other patients were wondering why I was there.

The room would soon become a haven for me, but sometimes a

curse. In this room patients might sit around during free time to talk or watch TV, as well as eat their meals. Here I would get to know the other patients informally, and sometimes learn more about myself.

I tried to show no emotion, but I was afraid. It was the first morning I would have to eat without being allowed to go straight to the bathroom to throw up. And I would not have a chance to get pink pills to swallow.

A nurse approached me as I picked up my breakfast tray. She said, "You'll have to stay in the day room an hour after you eat." So here was my first test. What should I do? Not eat, or eat and bear the burden of not getting rid of it? My monster was beginning to scream.

Elizabeth sat down with me, and a small woman joined us. Elizabeth said, "Hey, Cynthia, Brenda, here, is bulimic too." I almost wanted to shout with delight. Another one like me! Brenda and I stared at each other. I wanted her in my life no matter what. Not once in the past twelve years had I met another person with bulimia, and here in front of me was someone who could relate to me.

Brenda and Elizabeth pointed out other patients to me. "Clint is an alcoholic. The little girl over there is in for 'divorcing' her parents. Steven is in for depression. Carrie is anorexic and then she turned bulimic. That lady tried to kill herself." I knew in this day room my soul would awaken to feelings I'd never before imagined.

After breakfast Dr. Gutierrez, a psychiatrist, walked into the day room. He looked at me compassionately. "Hello, Cynthia. May I talk with you?"

We went into a small room. I was scared. That day I would be meeting all the members of my therapy team as I began each part of the therapy program, which would constitute most of my schedule for the next ten weeks of hospitalization.

"Tell me about your bulimia," the doctor said.

I told Dr. Gutierrez that I started purging at age seventeen, hardly eating anything, then popping laxative gum and throwing up. Actually, I had begun binging during the previous year, when I was a high school senior. It was an upsetting year for me, because I moved with my parents from my childhood home, Portland, Oregon, to

Oklahoma City. I started overeating for comfort, and gained about ten pounds that year. My dad offered me $300 if I would lose it for college. I took the bet, and a girlfriend told me, "Stop eating for two days a week and then, when you do eat, stick your finger down your throat . . . or take laxatives, and believe me, you can lose weight fast." So that summer, young and not knowing any better, I started my new diet. After a year the addiction took over. I kept thinking that if I could only be thin, my parents and other people would love and accept me.

"I've been doing it for twelve years; first weekly, then twice a week, and finally every day. I can't stop fasting, binging, and purging," I told the doctor. "I throw up at least four times a week."

"How many laxatives do you take?"

"Anywhere from thirty to a hundred a day."

He looked at me intently. "I am amazed you are alive!"

"I am, too. Six weeks ago I almost died. I hadn't eaten all day. I wanted to lose weight, so I took thirty laxatives on an empty stomach. I would have taken sixty pills, but I didn't have them. The next morning I couldn't move. My right side was numb. I couldn't hear with my right ear. Horrible cramps engulfed my body from neck to toes. I literally crawled to the phone. I took thirty minutes to get down my hall. I stopped often, because when I moved slightly I was sure I would die. Suddenly my fingers turned blue. I called a friend and she rushed me to her doctor. He gave me a sedative and said it was nerves, even though I told him I had bulimia."

"Cynthia, get ready," Dr. Gutierrez warned. "You are an over-the-counter drug addict and a food addict, and your body will soon go into shock. You won't be taking any more laxatives, and I am putting you on a strict three-meals-a-day nutritious diet."

My mind screamed, "But Doctor, I will get fat. Please don't do that."

Dr. Gutierrez saw the terror in my eyes. "You must give up the destructive control. You will learn that here."

"Control? What do you mean by control?" I thought.

"I will see you tomorrow, Cynthia. Tests will be run on you to see how your body is functioning. You're lucky to be alive."

Later I learned that my electrolyte level was so low that my life was indeed in danger when I entered the hospital.

Electrolytes are elements such as sodium, potassium, and chlorides that convey the body's electrical impulses. A low enough potassium level, for example, can cause the heart to stop beating. Electrolyte imbalance is a serious threat to the bulimic's life, as it occurs because of excessive vomiting over a prolonged period of time.

"All I know is that I want desperately to die, but I also want to live."

"If you work, it will happen."

Now, Dr. Gutierrez, whose eyes radiated love and compassion, gave me my first glimmer of hope behind those locked doors.

3

You're Going To Save Me?

When Mike Moore walked into the day room, I thought, "He's my therapist? He's overweight! No way can he help me. But, Jan said he will save my life." Mike was cool, calculating. I said hello and we went into a room to talk.

"How long can you be here, Cynthia?" Mike asked.

"Six weeks, and that's it. And I don't want to talk about anything else except me," I blurted. "I am twenty-eight years old. My parents are perfect. They are wonderful parents. It's me. And I have to hurry back to work."

His eyes seemed to be laughing at me. "Looking at your records, I see you have been binging, purging, and fasting for twelve years. Tell me more about your background, as far back as you can remember."

"Well, basically my life has been wonderful. I went to a private school in Portland, Oregon. I was popular. I went to college, went with a guy for three years, and we got married. It lasted only four months and we divorced. I pursued my career, and a week ago I wanted badly to blow my brains out. I can't put up with my life any longer, and this is my last chance to learn how to live."

"Okay," Mike said. "Tonight I want you to write me everything you remember about your life. Have it ready for me by tomorrow."

I left the room wondering if this man could possibly save me. He didn't like me, so how could he possibly understand me? But again, my soul whispered, "Hope, Cynthia."

Every day the patients took part in group therapy sessions. They lasted about ninety minutes and were usually led by Mike, with other staff people participating also. The purpose of group therapy was to give us an opportunity to develop relationships that were open and reciprocal, and that would provide mutual support. Here we were free to share our feelings and opinions about ourselves and about each other. Our problems were varied, but as we sat in a circle and I saw the tears and heard of the pain, I began to feel a common bond with the others in the group. However, my first time there I didn't know what to say.

I heard tales of abusive parents. A girl said she was raped. A man said he couldn't break down his wall. One man kept getting up and walking out, then coming in and interrupting everyone who talked. One girl, Carrie, cried while everyone talked. She hung her head down so low her hair covered her face. When she finally talked, she said all she wanted was for her parents to love her. Her dad always told her that because she was born, he didn't get all the material things he wanted. Why, if it weren't for her, he could have a swimming pool by now. She was in the way. As she told about her pain, she described my pain, too.

After everyone had walked out of the room, I told Carrie I needed to hug her. We held each other and cried. For so long, touching, feeling the warmth of a friend, hadn't felt good to me. Then, that morning when the nurse had touched my arm to take my blood pressure, I was relieved someone touched me. Just that simple touch of a fingertip gave me a sense of comfort. What had I done to myself, to have lost the need of a touch? Now my new friend was letting me know it was okay to hug, too.

"Why are you here, Carrie?" I asked.

"Oh, I lost seventy pounds and they made me gain it back. So I started eating, then taking laxatives."

"Then you are anorexic and bulimic?"

"Yes, I guess so."

"Your eyes are so sad, Carrie."

"Yours are too, Cynthia," she said.

My activities during my first few days in the hospital provided the staff with information that would help them evaluate my problem, as well as establish working relationships for my therapy.

Marta, the occupational therapist, was small, cute, and spunky, and I didn't like her personality. "Today we are going to do a body image," she told me.

"What's that?"

"You will go into a room and sit and look at yourself in a mirror, and you will write what you see. Here are some sheets of paper and a pencil, and in that room is a mirror. Close the door. You may have an hour to write."

My body? "Oh, please don't make me do this," I wanted to scream.

I sat down and the tears poured. "Oh, I hate you, Cynthia, I hate you. Look at you. You're an ugly fat slob. No self-control. You are nothing. You just ate lunch and the food will turn to fat. Fat, Cynthia, and you can't get rid of it here. You are so gross. I hate my face. I hate my chest. I hate my hips. I hate me," I wrote.

I started shaking; my mind was whirling, my head was killing me. "You're no good, Cynthia." I got up and ran out of the room. "I can't handle this, Marta."

"Okay. Why don't you go rest."

I handed her the hate-body-image paper. I went to my room and sobbed into my pillow.

Oh, dear God, I hate me. Why did you create me?

Occupational therapy became an important, though not always pleasant, part of the weeks that followed.

Since persons with eating disorders generally have distorted self-images, the occupational therapist supervises creative projects, such as crafts and clay sculpturing, which allow patients to nonverbally or symbolically express their feelings, to allow the body to be a means of commmunication in ways other than food-oriented expressions, and to enhance their self-images and interpersonal relationships.

Mike Moore did not talk to me about my bulimia, even though he knew it was basically a slow suicide. But his goals in the individual therapy sessions, which I had at least four times a week, were to help me explore my feelings, express my emotions, and to uncover the traumatic events in my life back to my childhood and the unresolved emotional conflicts which triggered and perpetuated my self-destructive behavior. These sessions were always intense and emotional and helped me to change my destructive behaviors.

We were together in a room with three chairs. I sat in one, and the other chairs were to represent people in my life, my feelings, or my attitudes. I sat down, scared, my arms folded tightly.

"What are you aware of?" Mike asked.

"I don't know."

"Let go, Cynthia. Let go."

Suddenly Mike's voice and the words *let go* penetrated my soul, and I felt a door opening. My eyes flooded with tears, and my body jerked with sobs. "I feel so empty. I feel nothing."

"Put him in the chair, Cynthia."

"Who?"

"Your dad. You know he's here. He's right here."

"My dad always told me, 'Cynthia, work out your own problems. Don't bother other people. Trust God and do it yourself.'"

"Look at your dad and say, 'This is my life. I am dying and I have to find out why. This is where I will find out why I want to die. This is my life, Dad.'"

Meekly I said, "This is my life, Dad."

"Yell, Cynthia. Yell it to your dad." Mike yelled to my dad in the chair, "I am dying and I want to save my life. I don't care what you think about it. I will talk to anyone about myself, because I don't want to die."

Then I screamed and raved. "This is my life, and I don't care what you think about it, Dad." The tears fell. That day I cried the tears that had been locked up for ten years. Suddenly I knew I was in the right place, with the man who would help me kill the monster.

So many tests were run on me—CAT scan, EEG, blood test, urine analysis—I thought maybe I had cancer and only two weeks to live. Or maybe I had a brain tumor and that's why I binged and purged and starved myself. I wished they would find something awfully wrong with me so I'd have an excuse for my horrid addiction.

The man who did my EEG acted nervous. After all, he did pick me up from the psychiatric ward. I tried to be friendly. "Will this test tell you if I am crazy?"

He didn't smile. "No, it will tell if anything is the matter with your brain chemicals."

I took a deep breath and he told me to be still. "Be still? Doesn't that mean be peaceful?" I thought. "Dear God, what is peace?"

After I returned to the ward Dr. Gutierrez came to see me and told me I had a bad vitamin deficiency. "That is the reason you are bruised all over. You'll have to take some heavy shots to get it back in control." He also put me on an antidepressant drug, plus fiber supplement, and stool softener.

"Dr. Gutierrez, I haven't gone to the bathroom in two days and my stomach feels awful. I can't stand being so puffy."

"It's going to take time," he said. "Your body has to adjust to your new way of life."

"My new way of life? All I want," I thought, "are those little pink pills to get rid of all the food I've eaten." Inside I felt the monster laughing, and wondered if Dr. Gutierrez noticed.

4

People

The following day I again listened to the sad people in my group. I felt much pain for them, or was it my own pain? Someone said that the group therapy room should be called the cry room.

That day I opened up, and my tears would not stop. Yet, I felt no comfort. When I could talk, I told about all the food I had been consuming and the ways I got rid of it. I told about the emptiness in my life. These people were listening, sharing my sorrow. It was as though I had opened a window, yet my soul was upset.

Mike had watched me all morning. After lunch I went to my room. As I looked out the window watching the rain, Mike walked in. His look frightened me. "What's going on, Cynthia?" he said.

"I'm afraid that a month won't be enough time to let me destroy the monster. I am so afraid I won't ever be a whole person again."

"Where's the hurt?"

"I don't know," I told Mike. But my heart was saying, "Daddy, why wasn't I ever good enough for you?" I wouldn't tell that to Mike, though.

"Think about where the hurt is." He turned and walked away.

The window was locked and barred, with no way to escape, but I didn't wish to escape. Drops of rain hit the glass. I could not touch the rain, but tears poured from the gray clouds of confusion, emptiness, pain, and sorrow within me. The sun might shine outside the next day, but inside my soul I didn't think it ever could.

An hour before I was to see Mike for individual therapy, my body began to feel shaky. I walked into the day room. A man named Steven, who sort of scared me, was sitting alone. He was over six feet tall and was skin and bones. His white face was sunken and his eyes were black, probably from lack of nutrition and sleep. His face showed sadness, or maybe violence. Though he frightened me, I wanted to talk to him, so I sat down. He noticed my hands shaking.

"What's going on, Cynthia?"

"I don't know. It must be the beginning of the withdrawals they warned me about."

"I know all about withdrawals."

"Oh?"

"Yes, I was a junkie for ten years. I did all the drugs. Then I quit about four years ago. I got completely free from all of that, but three weeks ago I broke down. I was so depressed I wanted to kill myself."

Steven's hair was curly black with touches of gray. He looked close to forty, but he told me he was twenty-eight. I couldn't believe it; Steven and I were the same age. Both of us wanted to die and neither knew why.

I liked Steven. He listened to me and seemed to care. I thought, "I want you for a friend, Steven. You're not like the rest of the men I have been around. You're not afraid of me, and you're even talking to me when I am so ugly and fat and no good."

Mike had his feet up on a chair as he looked over the autobiography I had written the evening before. He put his head back and sighed. "Hm-m. I see you were burned when you were four."

"Yes. It was no big deal. I was scared, but I don't remember much about it."

"And you have a brother. Robby is his name."

"Yes. We love each other, but I don't think we have ever liked one another. I was always the good little girl and he always disliked me for being the goody-goody."

"What does Robby do?"

"He makes a living selling ivory. His lifestyle is the opposite of mine. But he is a good guy. He nearly lost his leg four years ago. Some guy, high on drugs, got mad at him and was going to kill him, but instead shot his leg."

"What's your dad like?"

"Bold, aggressive, not scared of anything. Very optimistic about life. A firm believer in God. Big and tall—six foot, three."

"Your mom?"

"Tiny, timid, shy, kind, beautiful."

"This next week I want you to do some picture tests with Marta in occupational therapy," Mike said as he left. "See you tomorrow."

That evening there was a phone call for me. I wondered who knew I was there. It was Dad, and I didn't want to talk to him.

When I told him I was going to a hospital in Dallas, he reacted angrily, saying, "You don't have to quit your job. There has to be someone in Little Rock who can help you." I wanted to scream and tell him there was no one, and if I didn't go to Dallas I would die. But he'd never understand. The year before, when I told him I was taking sixty laxatives a day, he firmly said, "You do not!" So, I never said another word about it. If my dad wouldn't believe me, who would?

Now Dad was at the Dallas airport. "Well, are you settled in?"

"Sure, Dad," I wanted to say. "This day camp is wonderful. There's a swimming pool and I'm getting a great tan."

His voice was cheerful. Didn't he know his daughter had wanted to kill herself a week before?

We groped for words. I was relieved when he told me he'd be in touch but that he didn't suggest coming to see me. Yet, when I said good-bye, I became angry that he didn't ask if he could come out to the hospital to see me, and that I didn't get the chance to say, "Don't bother. I don't want to see you." Why was I never good enough for him?

That night I had nightmares about people from the past. I quivered inside, woke up crying, but couldn't move. My insides were falling apart, it seemed.

God, please help me.

On the fourth day I still couldn't bear seeing my image in the mirror, and wondered how in the world the people on the ward could stand to look at my fat face. But that day I started noticing people myself, and remembering more names.

There are about seven members of the nursing staff on each shift. They are an integral part of the treatment team, involved in the planning and evaluation of each patient's progress. At the beginning, a staff member is always with an eating-disorder patient, seeing to it she eats what is on her prescribed diet, accompanying her to the bathroom so she will not vomit, and being available to listen and help her through difficult times on the ward.

I liked an aide named Rachel. She was my age and told me she was going to be a psychiatrist. If I needed to talk, I was supposed to go to Rachel and she would listen to me.

An aide I disliked was Tye. He appeared to be the typical good-looking guy who loves the girls and then drops them. After each meal, he checked my platter for how much I had eaten, which irritated me. There were also nurses on each shift who seemed kind.

There were about fourteen people in my therapy group. Elizabeth, my roommate, was a lovely girl—tall, red-haired and freckled. She felt as if she was in prison, and was angry that her parents and her doctor had put her in the hospital. She hurriedly ate her meals, saying she just had to gain her weight to get out of there.

Elizabeth recalled days she wouldn't eat anything, "just starve myself and go jogging." She felt in control when she didn't eat, as if she were better than anyone else. Her parents seldom allowed her to do things with her friends. They controlled her, so she controlled them with anorexia.

Brenda was a small, blond, lively woman. She had been bulimic for fifteen years. She and her husband, an airline pilot, had been married twelve years and had two children. She had been on the ward for a month.

Whenever she went grocery shopping she would buy an extra bag of food to eat on the way home and then throw up when she got home. Her children were in school and her husband away much of the time. He never knew about her bulimia until recently, when it had overwhelmed her to the point of her having to tell him.

Randy was fourteen years old, six feet tall, and skinny. He kept his head down all the time. Two weeks before, he had taken 100 tranquilizers with a bottle of whiskey. He said that all he wanted out of life was to be loved by his mom and dad, but since they never touched him he thought they hated him. So he wanted to die.

Clint never smiled. His eyes betrayed his alcoholism. At breakfast someone told Clint I was a news reporter. He came over and said, "We haven't had anyone here with class. The first day you walked into the day room I thought you were a doctor. It was the way you walked and looked."

Class? A doctor? "Nope," I thought, "I am just a sick, fat, ugly woman wanting to kill myself."

Over the next few days Clint revealed that he was afraid of pain. So he put on a "John Wayne" act in order to survive. But deep down he was afraid and untrusting.

Clint owned a ranch, and one night when he was home on pass he beat up a man who came to see him. Years before, when a nurse was dressing an acid burn on his shoulder, he dared not show he was in almost unbearable pain.

One day I asked Clint, "Do you think you are good-looking?"

"When I was twenty, but now at thirty-four I'm washed out."

I told him he was handsome in a rugged way. "I think most people like men who aren't John Wayne. At least, I like men who show their tears and fears and hurts and smiles."

"So why don't you show yours?" he asked. "I don't understand why you are here, you look so strong."

Many of these people wished to die, and some actually were near death before coming to the hospital. I wondered if, when they left, they would again be alive within their souls.

After four days in the hospital I still hadn't had a bowel movement. My stomach was bloated and I despised the feeling of food in my stomach. I was worried about getting fat and wondering if I could hold out to the end of my hospital program.

A nurse assured me that even though my body was in shock, with time—perhaps several days—it would adjust. I hit my stomach and looked out the window. It was still raining outside, and inside me.

God, stay with me. Please help my abused body. I need you; don't leave me. Give me your hand to hold on to. Hold on to mine, tight. I need you tonight.

5

Withdrawal

When I awakened the fifth morning, I could barely move. All night long my body had quivered unbearably. Elizabeth told me to hurry because breakfast had come. I floundered to the bathroom and didn't dare look in the mirror.

I turned on the water, without thinking put my hand into it, and reeled from the shock. The water stung my skin! I couldn't bear the touch of mere water. I screamed and fell to my knees. My body was shaking all over. "Please, somebody help me!"

A nurse came in and knew immediately what was happening. "It's withdrawal, Cynthia. The laxatives have had a numbing effect, and now as it gets back to normal, your body is going to put you through agony for a while." So, now that I had gone "cold turkey," I would be sensitive to everything.

"Please, let me go to bed."

"No, you have to get used to this." The nurse helped me get dressed. I got to group therapy late, but didn't hear a word. My shakes were unbearable.

Later in the day, Dr. Gutierrez said I might go outside for a short time. After five days inside it should be good for me. It wasn't. I don't think I have ever been so frightened in my life. I walked out with Katie, an aide. My legs felt like jelly.

The outdoors scared me. I wanted to scream. The sunlight hurt my eyes. The slight breeze hit my face and seemed to cut me like a knife. What was wrong with my body?

Katie pointed to a tiny purple flower growing near the walk. I didn't care. I could have reached down and picked that flower, but I didn't deserve to see that beauty. My tears fell. I didn't tell Katie I felt worthless, but asked her to take me back inside.

I returned to my room sobbing, and told Elizabeth to leave me alone.

An hour later I walked into the day room. Randy was there and I started telling him how awful I had felt outdoors. I was so frightened. "Oh, Randy, what is wrong with me?" He put his arms around me. "I'm so scared."

"I am too, Cynthia." He told me his parents were searching for a boys' institution for him to live in. Randy didn't want to go, nor to leave the friends he had made in the hospital. All he wanted was a family with a real mom and dad to love him. I loved this little boy who had much kindness and understanding.

That evening my mom called me. I was angry at her and Dad; yet, I was also angry at myself. I had embarrassed them. Their daughter was in a psychiatric ward. What would people think? I had failed them. Still, it was my life.

Mom had just returned from a trip to the coast. I didn't really want to talk to her. "How are you, Mom?"

"Oh, I'm sick. I think I ate some bad fish and I've been throwing up."

I wanted to scream, "So what? Here I am in a psychiatric ward fighting for my life and you are nauseated!"

"Are you all right?" Mom continued. "Are you settled in? Have they put you on a good diet?"

Oh, that comment cut deeply. I wanted to rave, "Is that all that matters, Mom, a good diet? A good figure? Yes, they have me fasting so I will finally be so thin you will love me."

But I didn't say anything. I got off the phone as quickly as I could and ran to my room sobbing. "All they care about is my body. It's like they think I'm at a fat farm, a spa, when I am in a *psychiatric ward!*"

Memories of my TV days flashed through my mind. Every time I planned to go home to see my parents, I would hardly eat a thing for days, and when I did, I would take my laxatives and throw up. I knew the first thing my dad would say when I walked in the door would be, "Oh, Cynthia, you've lost weight, haven't you? You look good." Or, if I had put on some weight, he would say, "Your face is a little puffy, dear. Have you been eating too many doughnuts?"

I would want to shout, "What about me, the me inside?"

The nurse who had come into my room said, "If your parents upset you so much, why don't you write them and ask them to leave you alone for a while?"

Good idea. I wrote: "Dear Mom and Dad, You don't understand what I am going through. I don't want to see you or talk to you for a while. Leave me alone. Your daughter, Cynthia."

During the night I awakened from a vivid dream. In the dream, my mom and I were at a restaurant. I watched what I ate. After lunch, I went to pay the bill and my mom went to the rest room. I hurriedly grabbed about ten candy bars and started gobbling them. I looked back, and my mom was watching with a disapproving look. I just laughed. Somehow we met a sexy-looking man. My mom, he, and I ended up at his house. Leaving my mom in the living room, the man and I went to his bedroom to make love. My mom knew what was going on. After our love scene, I walked into the living room and laughed. Then I woke up!

I was so shocked by that dream, I got up to talk to an aide. "I would never do that, Joe. But it was so real."

"You're angry, Cynthia. That was a dream of rebellion."

"Yes, I did everything my mom is opposed to. Her phone call made me so angry. Here I am in the hospital fighting for my life and she tells me she has a stomach ache. All my life, that's all I've heard. She is always sick. When I was a kid, I would come home after school to a dark house, and Mom would be in bed, sick with ulcers. She has always been sick, but now I am sick. I want to give up on life. Why can't they understand, Joe?"

"Give them time. Maybe they will understand; but if they won't, you will have to learn to accept that."

Candy was the fourteen-year-old who had "divorced" her parents. She had been swearing in group therapy the eleven weeks of her hospital stay. When I confronted her, the first person in the group to do so, Steven turned on me. He said my calling her a punk was too hostile and critical.

I told Candy I was sorry I had hurt her, but repeated that her vulgarity offended me. "You have so much, Candy. You don't have to be tough." She forgave me, but it didn't matter. I didn't think I deserved to be forgiven. I cried.

As I walked to my room, Steven yelled down the hall, "Hey, Cynthia, we've forgiven you; now forgive yourself."

I wanted to reply, "I can't forgive myself, Steven. I am no good." For my striking out at Candy had brought back memories of my dad yelling at Robby, telling him he was dumb. That, in turn, reminded me of my sitting at the breakfast table eating an over-easy egg on toast, the yolk running down over my fingers or on to my plate, and my dad yelling at me, "Look at you! You look like a slob. Now get up and wipe the mess off your hand."

Later, Mike came to my room and told me to relax and close my eyes. Mike said, "You have many memories locked deep inside you. While you are in the hospital, allow yourself to feel safe enough to unlock them. You are here to find out why you wished to die. Free yourself of the control of those secrets that make you self-destructive."

"But I hate myself," I thought. "I hate my body, I feel so big. My

bowels haven't moved in eight days. I am so angry. I sit down to eat
and hate the food. Yet, I am so hungry. But the food is awful, food I
never eat. I want my pink pills."

Brenda, Carrie, and I were together talking about our binges and
purges. Carrie said that after starving herself, she had to gain weight
and so started eating everything. Her binges were in the early morning
hours, when she devoured huge bags of chocolate candy and then
took one hundred laxatives. It turned out that Carrie and I, by process
of elimination, had come up with the same combination of drug-
counter laxatives.

I told about the nights after work when I would stop at three
different drive-ins and get three huge ice cream cones at each stop, a
total of nine cones on the way home. Sometimes I would order three
hamburgers too, and after each stop take the pills. Then I would
consume any food in my house, thawing frozen food with hot water
or hurriedly gobbling food straight from the can. For the next two or
three days I wouldn't eat anything. I drank water and coffee and
made myself run before and after work.

Brenda said, "Sometimes I would bake a cake and eat the whole
thing. But I would make sure I had another cake mix and immediately bake the second cake so that my family would never find out."

Elizabeth joined us. Her eating problem was just the opposite. She
never ate. At the family dinner table she would take a bite of food
and put her napkin to her mouth to get rid of the unchewed food.
She would cook gourmet meals, which her parents thought she did
for the pleasure of eating. But her obsession with staying thin caused
her to not touch a bite.

We four had in common our desperate need to get rid of our
monsters.

6

Damaged Freight

Mike gave a lecture on anger which gave me new insights into how my parents and I handled anger.

Dad was the aggressive one; Mom was passive. When my dad was angry he screamed and yelled. It didn't matter what the rest of us thought, because he gave us no choice. Mom never expressed her anger. Possibly keeping anger to herself contributed to her having stomach ulcers.

Mike explained that aggressive anger is a person's attempt to overcome feelings of inferiority, and to control other people without caring about their feelings. Passive anger is a recoiling from a situation, or an attempt to accept it. The messages I received while growing up as to how I should handle my own anger were confusing. I didn't know how to control my anger because I hated both the aggressive and passive kinds, so I suppressed anger and then comforted myself with food.

For example, if at work I was angry with a photographer for not getting the shots I needed, I would maybe yell at him. But usually I wouldn't say a thing, run upstairs, shove twelve candy bars down my throat, then get rid of them. It was as though my binge and purge were symbolic: stuffing down the food dealt with the anger, and purging myself of the food purged me of the anger. At the same time, I was in control and didn't hurt anyone's feelings; after all, if I showed anger, the other person might not like me.

But I learned from Mike about a better way to deal with anger, using assertive anger, which says, "I need, I feel, I want, I think, and even if I don't get what I want, at least I expressed my anger with maturity." I felt a tremendous sense of freedom from some invisible bond when I realized how my parents and I had handled anger. I wondered if I could change.

Clint and Candy sat next to me my tenth day in group therapy. I sensed that people who didn't care much about me at first now wanted to be near me, and I wanted to be near them. We were like the people in the outside world who didn't understand me nor I them, but slowly we were learning.

Mike got Candy to tell about "that scared little girl." When Candy was three her mother terrorized her, and she jumped through a glass window to wet ground two stories below. She was only shaken, but no one came to pick her up. The thought that *no one came* struck a new chord in my being.

In my individual therapy sessions Mike kept asking me where my hurt was coming from. "I don't know," I cried. I had memories of being thrown into boiling water, Mom being home alone with us children, terror in Robby's face.

Mike asked, "When did you become damaged freight, Cynthia?"

"After my divorce," I answered. "I was only nineteen. After my four-month marriage I was alone. People reacted to me differently. The church guys wouldn't be my friends because I was divorced."

But Mike said, "Are you sure the feeling of being damaged freight didn't begin years before that?"

Somewhere my thoughts were crying, "Daddy, Daddy, why wasn't I good enough for you?" But I didn't want to talk about Dad. I hadn't lived with Mom and Dad for over seven years, and I wouldn't allow myself to betray my parents by telling Mike the repressed feelings I had toward them.

One evening Clint came into the day room and we talked about a poem he wrote. I thought he took me seriously. We were interrupted by the phone, but before I went to bed, he told me he really wanted to finish talking to me. I asked the "John Wayne" to punch me on the arm. Instead, he said, "How about a hug? I need a hug." It felt right hugging Clint, my new friend.

Randy, my tall, skinny fourteen-year-old friend, was having a hard time. Dr. Gutierrez had told him he was going home to his parents. But then the plans changed when they decided to put him in a home for delinquent boys. Randy became enraged, messed up the nursing station, and pulled a phone out of the wall. That evening he told me that if he didn't go back to his parents, he'd find a way to die.

The next morning when he came into the group, his eyes were swollen from much crying. He announced, "I am leaving and I want to say good-bye to my friends."

I began shaking and weeping. When Randy came to me, he had to comfort me. I told him, "Please believe in yourself. Believe you are worthwhile."

After Randy left the room, Mike turned to me and said, "You seem to be in more pain than Randy."

"All he wants is love and attention," I replied.

Mike said, "Like you, Cynthia? Say, 'All I want is love and attention.' Say it, Cynthia."

I couldn't because I was sobbing too much to talk. When I calmed down I told Clint his hug the night before meant very much to me, but I wondered why he wanted to hug *me*.

"You underestimate yourself," Mike said, and asked me why I felt that way.

I answered, "Because I have met lots of Clints and wanted them to know me, but I was always too big, too assertive."

Clint said, "I care about everyone in this room." Then he pointed a finger at me, saying, "That one—I talk to her for five minutes and want to start crying."

My tears wouldn't stop, Mike looked hard at me and told me to share the experience of being burned at age four. "Tell them, Cynthia. Tell us about loneliness."

Something clicked. I was no longer in that circle of people. I broke, sobbing, and relived a past event I didn't know still lived in me. There I was with my brother, bouncing up and down on the bed. There was a push, and suddenly my body was being flooded with a gallon of boiling water, water that was bubbling in a vaporizer. Robby and I had bad colds, so the water had been boiling all night. The push, the boiling water falling on me, the screams, the four-year-old girl running all over the house—I was on fire! "Mom, Mom, where are you? Dad, Dad, where are you?"

I heard screams again. Were they mine? Suddenly the circle of people was staring at me. I was rocking. Brenda had tears in her eyes. Mike asked her what she was feeling. Brenda said, "I want to hold her."

Mike said, "Then do it."

Brenda came to me and held me. I cradled in her arms like a baby. My sobs wouldn't quit. My eyes wouldn't open. Then someone else was holding me, patting me. It was Mike. Why would Brenda and Mike want to comfort me?

I skipped lunch and went to bed. My mind couldn't comprehend what had happened. A fear within shook me. The monster, it seemed, was rattling its chains.

Steven was having a painful time in the group sessions. When Mike asked him what he was aware of, he could only say he felt empty. Mike made him close his eyes. "What do you see, Steven?"

"A window."

"What kind of window?"

"Grey-colored window."

"What else do you see, Steven?"

"I see me looking through it, and then there is my daughter, my ex-wife, and my girlfriend. They have their hands up on the window trying to get through. My ex-wife is laughing. My little girl is crying. She is screaming for me. My girlfriend is crying. And I can't get the window open. I am trying but I can't. I am even trying to break it, but I can't. It won't break."

Steven was sweating and shaking. When he could no longer bear what he saw, he opened his eyes.

Mike blinked, and said, "What's going on, Steven?"

"I don't know. I feel so helpless. I don't feel anything." Steven is sad. He cannot connect his heart with his mind. He is very analytical, very intelligent. He can't seem to show emotion. He wanted to cry but he couldn't. A thought came to me. The sweat around his face and eyes and beard were like teardrops. I thought, "Steven, you really are crying."

When the aide, Rachel, looked at me, I knew she was concerned about me. Rachel seemed older and wiser than I, yet we were the same age. She was always asking how I felt about men. How could I know? It had been two years since I was involved in a relationship with a man. She asked if I was mad that bulimia only seems to afflict women. I wasn't. Rachel said she liked me because I was strong (I was sick of being strong), and told me I was working hard. I said I had to work hard; if I didn't, I would die.

During one strange therapy session, Mike persuaded me to relax. Then he said, "I want you to picture having a wedding."

I told him, "All I see is a black void."

He said, "I will stay here all day until you imagine it."

Nothing came. Wait, there was an outdoor wedding. My dad was there, and other people. But the groom and I weren't there. "I can't, Mike. Nothing comes up in my mind."

"Okay, then, picture your honeymoon. You and your groom will be there, and your honeymoon will be wonderful."

Nothing came into my mind. No one was there, not even me. "I can't, Mike. I see nothing, feel nothing."

"Interesting," Mike said. And as he often did, he abruptly left the room before I could say any more.

Lord, are you there? Do you have some time, Lord, to listen to me? Things are happening, and I am scared. What does it all mean? Each new day I am grasping new feelings, feelings I didn't know existed. God, have a reason for this pain that is being aroused. Please get me through this journey, help me learn why I have done what I have done. Please set me free. And, God, if you would, please move these bowels. I can't take it much longer.

A day short of my having been in the hospital two weeks I had my first visitor, my cousin Diana. I don't know what she must have thought when she saw me. She cried when we embraced.

The previous April, Di and her babies were in their house when a tornado hit. It was a miracle they all lived. I recalled the weekend I went to visit her. Her body was broken, but she was happy to be alive. My own spirit was broken, my life meaningless. I wished I could change places with her, that I had been hurt.

Now she was telling me that, even though God had put her through all the pain, she was still happy to be alive. I loved Diana. I wanted to live as she did, with thankfulness. But I wondered if it would ever happen.

Dr. Gutierrez told me that, fortunately, I had done no extensive damage to my body. My stomach lining was scarred, my vitamin deficiency would have to be monitored, but I was over the dangerously low potasium level I had when I came to the hospital, which could have caused me to die. My bowels still hadn't moved after two weeks.

"Please, Dr. Gutierrez, I cannot take this."

"We'll give you an enema tonight. I see your hands are shaking," he said.

"Yes, my shakes won't go away."

"Give it time."

That evening the nurse gave me three enemas. They didn't work. What was wrong? The next step was castor oil. I took it. It was awful, but if it worked, I didn't care what it tasted like.

Mom and Dad called, and I could tell they were beginning to sense the reality of having a sick child in a psychiatric ward, but I still felt hostile toward them. Dad asked me if I wanted the church members to know I was sick. Did I want cards?

"That's okay." They told me they loved me. I crawled into bed feeling lost and alone.

I am so frighened, God. I thank you for making sure I didn't do any extensive damage to my body, but please make my bowels start to work again. God, the outside world scares me. I feel safe here, but I am scared of never getting well. Please help me. Stay with me. See me through this.

7

Clint

After breakfast, Clint came to talk to me. I felt safe with him around, but it was a new feeling that frightened me. He told me that before he came to the hospital all he did was drink, but he held a good engineering job. On the way to work he would drink a bottle of bourbon and he always had a thermos of alcohol with him. His wife brought him to the hospital drunk. I asked what she was like and he said she was unfaithful. Clint had been there three months, and he knew when he got out of the hospital he would fail.

If he felt that way, would I fail when I got out? I couldn't go back to binge eating and purging. I must *destroy* my monster. I looked at Clint and said, "If you leave without getting well, you'll let us all down. Don't leave us while you're still sick, my friend."

Clint didn't want to go to group therapy, but I told him, "Look, if you don't find out what you're afraid of, you'll never know how to get on with life." I asked him to go for me. He went and the whole group session was focused on him.

Mike asked him to remember when he was eight years old. Clint closed his eyes and said he saw a well. He started shaking and crying, a sudden change that was frightening. The little boy believed the devil lived in the well. His granddaddy picked him up and held him by the ankles, then started to drop Clint inch by inch, head first, into the dark well.

Clint started screaming, "Don't, Granddaddy! Please, don't!"

With a laugh, his granddaddy said, "I'm going to drop you down into this well where the devil lives, boy. You belong to the devil. You don't belong to me."

Tears rolled out of Clint's eyes. Tears of sadness and anger poured out of the eyes of all of us in the room. We all wanted to rescue that scared little boy. Mike made us stand up and surround Clint. Mike told us to touch Clint and patch up the well. Clint's whole body was shaking. He thought he was going to faint, but he wouldn't allow us to get rid of the devil and the well. Clint wouldn't let us, his friends, rescue him.

Clint avoided me after the session, so I wrote him this letter. "Clint: You went to group for yourself, not me. I know you believe that, in a way, I made you go and you feel awful, tortured, because you did. But, Clint, we've got to feel tortured and relive all the nightmares before we can learn to handle the outside world, to understand why we are so afraid. We must feel the emptiness and pain before we can be healed. We all wanted to fill that well. You wouldn't let us. I wonder, would you be 'John Wayne' enough to fill my wells? Would you please allow Clint, the real Clint, to reach out and grab on to hope? Cynthia."

Mike asked me whom on the staff I did not like. I told him the aide, Tye, and the occupational therapist, Marta.

"Why?"

"Because Tye to me is the typical jerk. He wouldn't have a thing to do with me if I knew him outside. You know, a-kiss-the-girls-and-leave-them type of guy. And Marta is too high spirited, too cocky for me."

"Go tell them that," Mike said.

"What?"

"Today, you are to go and tell them how you feel about them."

First I found Marta. It's not too easy to say, "I don't feel good around you." If I didn't like people I usually just avoided them.

Marta said, "Why?"

I told her that I thought she didn't really care about me. "That's okay, but you work here. You're supposed to help me, not like me."

Marta got a piece of paper and said, "Draw me."

I proceeded to draw her. I am not an artist, but I did the best I could. She looked like a tomboy to me.

After I had finished, she said, "That's me? I look like a man."

"Well, a tomboy, at least."

"All you have drawn is a face, hair, shirt, and pants. Where is the rest of me? And where are my earrings?"

"I don't know! I never noticed you had a chest. You cover it up with those big shirts. And your earrings are so small. I didn't notice them."

I then found Tye. I said, "I have a problem with you and I need to figure out why. I don't like you. You make me angry every time I am around you. For one thing, you pay attention only to the young patients. You never talk or make an effort to get to know the older ones, and I am one of those. Basically, I feel you are a jerk."

"Why?"

"You just remind me of all the jerks out there who don't want women with intelligence and an on-the-ball attitude. You look like someone who would only go for tiny, phony women."

"Well, Cynthia, you're wrong. I never had one-night stands with anyone. In fact, I just broke up with a lady I went with for three years. And as far as my getting to know the kids here, that's true. I happen to enjoy kids. But you're right; my job is to help everyone here. Now that you have criticized me, let me ask you a few questions. Did you ever date on the outside?"

"Rarely, because all the men I knew were scared of me. I am tall and aggressive and I know where I am going. I guess they don't. I got sick of being intimidating to men so I just gave up on ever finding one for me. I also quit dating because I couldn't handle the games of playing hard-to-get. Two years ago, I went with a man for six months. I really did care for him. I was even willing to give up my career and move to California where he had a new job, but it didn't work out."

"Why?"

"Well, the main thing was that he was an atheist. But I went away for three weeks to Singapore before he was to leave, and during that time he decided he didn't love me enough to marry me. I knew he wouldn't be good for me for the rest of my life, but I loved him."

Tye looked at me, and I could tell he was ready to deliver some smart comment, and he did. "I have noticed that you associate only with certain people here; like the only people I see you with are Clint and Brenda, and sometimes Steven."

"So, what if I want to know only three people?"

"But," Tye argued, "I wonder if that's what you do on the outside— have a select few friends."

"So, what if I do? I don't want the whole world knowing about my life."

"Well, think about this. What you do on the outside, you want to change here inside."

Tye left. I did not like that guy. Friends? Who needed them? I had no one and wanted no one.

Well, I had one friend. She told me I was her best friend. I didn't know why. She had it all: money and a great career. She called me and told me everyone at work missed me. I said, "Who? Who has asked about me?" She had to admit no one had asked about me. A voice inside said to me, "Isn't it sad, Cynthia, that you have been away from work for two weeks and no one knows or cares?"

Mike wanted to see me that day. It was my sixteenth day there. "What would you say if I told you that you had to stay here longer than a month?"

I said, "If that's what it will take, okay. My insurance will run out. But maybe I can ask my church for a loan."

Clint did a lot of talking in the next group session. I got sick to my stomach. He told tales about how his grandparents treated him. Clint's mom and dad died in a car wreck when he was two and his grandparents raised him. His mother was full-blooded Indian, so his grandfather called him a halfbreed. Clint was not allowed to eat at the table while growing up, but ate on the floor next to the table. Many days his grandpa would take him to the well and say, "You belong in there with the devil, boy."

The more Clint talked, the more my stomach churned. I had to run to the bathroom. The combination of castor oil and nerves did something to me, and I had a bowel movement. A real bowel movement! In twelve years I had not had a natural bowel movement. "Oh, praise the Lord!" I laughed as nature took over.

Mike came to my room. I guess he thought I was skipping group therapy. I wanted to jump and shout, "Mike, I had a b.m." But being the mature woman I was I refrained from doing so.

Back in the group Mike made me close my eyes and pretend I was talking to my brother. The tears and sobs came, and memories of Robby being in trouble, Mom crying, voices, yelling, screaming, and me—alone. I looked at one of the chairs and put Dad in it. "Oh, Daddy, all Robby wants is for you to stay home. All he wants is love." Suddenly, I felt that loneliness. I closed my eyes and Mike asked me what I was thinking. "I see that little girl. She is scared of all the screams and the crying. No one comes to her, so she is running out of the house. She is so lonely." All I could think was, "Daddy, Daddy, Robby embarrassed you and out of your own guilt you had to punish your son." Poor Dad, poor Robby, sad Cynthia.

I was going to my room when Clint handed me a letter. I sat on my bed and read it.

"Dear Cynthia, I find it extremely difficult to get your face and eyes out of my mind. I enjoy very much sharing my true feelings with you. It's scary to me, admitting that to you, but don't ask me why. I think the reality of finally meeting someone I can share genuine feelings with is too much for my mind to comprehend. I love spending time and talking with you. Conversation between us never gets old. It just gets better. I'd like to have the opportunity to spend some time with you in private, but I know you're not comfortable with that. I have respect for your moral codes. I want you to be comfortable when you're with me. As for me, I am happy to be with you regardless of the circumstances, I have come to the conclusion that whatever this is between you and me is worth some effort. Who knows, the Lord works in mysterious ways. Feeling and believing you care a little for me feels good. I want to hold you so badly. I hope that some day this will be possible. I need your touch, nobody else will do. Whatever it is you have on me is very new to me, frightening yet confusing, but wonderful. I'm looking forward to our future time spent together. You're a special lady. Love, Clint."

What was going on here? I wasn't sure about all this, but I felt good, a feeling that didn't come to me often.

I went to the day room and Clint was there. When he was in the room, something happened to me, and I didn't want to leave. I felt safe when he was there. He said, "Why is there always electricity when I am near you? Why did you come here, Cynthia? You scare me."

Candy came over and Clint talked about buying his little girl dresses. Then I had to leave the room. He had a child! What was happening? I didn't want to get hurt.

I was awake much of the night. What was I supposed to do, where must I go, who was I supposed to be? I was afraid of not finding the answers here. I wanted to talk, but everyone was asleep. The nurse I wanted had the night off, and I couldn't just go to Clint and say, "I need you."

God, why do you punish me? I know you "knitted me in my mother's womb" (Psalm 139), but for what purpose, for whose gain? I am confused, sad, unfulfilled. I want a man to love me and stay with me, children. But God, I am so overbearing, so ugly, so big, who would want me? Help me find a solution to this loneliness.

8

Men

The aide, Rachel, asked me the next morning why I was crying. I told her how alone I was the night before, when everyone was asleep. I remembered that happening in college. My boyfriend, Matthew, my love, would take me to the dorm at curfew. I hated leaving him. I would cry and cry, then binge and purge. My best friend would be asleep and I didn't want to bother her. Now I didn't want to bother anyone, either. Carrie told me I should have awakened her. Brenda said the same. Clint only stared at me.

After lunch, I asked Clint what he felt like when we had talked the previous evening. He said, "I wanted to hold you all night. That's all." I didn't tell him, but I too wanted that, even though it was wrong.

We were sitting by the window in the day room. I purposely avoided the sun shining in my face so Clint wouldn't see my scars and ugliness. He echoed my thoughts. "I don't want you to see the sunshine on this dusty trailed face." He had a lot of lines around his eyes, lines of pain and sorrow and abuse. My Clint, my friend, the big-city girl and the cowboy, worlds apart. Would our worlds ever come together?

Saturday many of my friends left on passes. I still might not leave, because the staff didn't trust me not to go right to the store and get pink pills. Clint left without saying good-bye, which I couldn't understand. I missed him even before he left.

In the evening I ate five big oatmeal cookies, snacks for the patients. I felt guilty I'd lost control, and had to get rid of the food. But Sally, a nice nurse, talked to me and watched me like a hawk. I couldn't go to the bathroom without her. "Oh, Sally, why did I do it? They are awful cookies."

"It's done, Cynthia," she said. "So forgive yourself." Forgive myself? It was so hard.

Sunday I read a book that talked about reasons for suffering, the Book of Job. My cousin, Di, and her husband came to see me. After five minutes with them I was tired. I tired so easily.

I watched the clock all day, anxious for Brenda and Clint to return. Brenda came back at 5:30, but Clint was late. He came into the group with a cowboy hat and sunglasses, dirty and sweating. After the session he told me he'd worked with his chickens all day. I asked him why he hadn't said good-bye. He said it wasn't time yet to say good-bye.

I couldn't sleep, and during the night Joe, the aide, and I talked for a couple hours about God. "It's so hard to know what he wants," I said. "It's so hard to pray."

Joe suggested I pray about changing my values. He had a point. I had been so concerned about my body image. I lost sight of everything else. Joe made me some hot chocolate, but I still didn't sleep.

The next morning Clint wrote me a letter:

"Dear Cynthia, As I attempt to write this, I'm feeling very awestruck to be communicating with you on paper. I really haven't been able to pinpoint exactly what it is about you that is able to reach into me. I share things with you that nobody else knows. Why? Sometimes, I can see into your mind but I'm afraid to look. I like sharing with you but that scares me too. I don't want to love you. I don't even want to like you, but I still do. I want to leave you but I don't want you to leave me and that doesn't make sense. You confuse me and make me enjoy it at the same time. It's difficult for me to look right into your eyes. The little electricity thing is there. Please understand. Clint."

In group therapy, Clint talked about his wife. She is jealous of his progress. He said she runs around on him, but he'll let her stay. I hurt bad after that.

In the mail were about ten letters for me. Some made me cry, especially the one from Mom:

"Darling, We received your letter today. We love you and are not ashamed of you being there, but rather deeply thankful you have found a place that will help you. Dad and I pray constantly for your recovery. We have been digging and studying everything we can on bulimia. We went to the library and did research. We love you so very much. Mom."

And there was a letter from Jan, the lady who urged me to enter the hospital.

"Dear Cynthia, You will never know how much my thoughts and prayers have been with you. I know by now you are feeling pain. But be encouraged by that pain. To feel pain means you will find the answers to why you were punishing yourself. I hope by now the pain of not taking the laxatives has lessened. I can truly understand the feeling of overwhelming frustration at mealtime. I know since you have started working with Mike you are probably experiencing more pain. But time and work and a sincere effort is making recovery possible for you. Trust Mike. He is a special blessing to us both. It is not always for us to understand the ways and will of God. I, too, have felt very angry at his slowness to meet my needs. But pray for God's will concerning you. I pray that he will work through Mike and the staff. God is so alive and so active. Just think of the indirect way he had me let you know there is hope. He wants you there. He is in control and I feel so good about that. There is a whole world out here, far from food and thoughts of food. It's filled with people and nature and fulfilling goals for each of us. I pray for your freedom. I love you. Jan."

Dear Jan. I had seen her only once, yet it seemed we had known each other a lifetime.

My head was hurting, my hands wouldn't stop shaking. When would these withdrawals be over? The letters kept coming to me, but when I sat down to write, I got so shaky, I couldn't write. When would I be normal?

In occupational therapy Marta said I could do anything, so I painted lots and lots of hearts, mostly black. Inside the hearts I put black tears, and then I hooked all the hearts together with lines.

Marta looked at the hearts and said, "What's going on?"

"That's how I feel. I feel so broken, like my insides are all apart and nothing connects. My life is in pieces and I don't know how to get all these hearts made into one."

Marta looked at me strangely. "I don't know how long you have, Cynthia, but from the looks of this picture, I hope you have a long time here."

My longing for Clint was getting stronger. But he was beginning to avoid me. Why was I so attracted to the man? I didn't dare tell anyone. What would Mike do if he knew? I didn't trust Mike enough to tell him yet. I knew I had to think out loud with Mike to get over my agony, but I couldn't trust him 100 percent yet. It was difficult to trust God 100 percent, too.

Our group kept changing as people left the hospital and new ones came in. One woman had cut her wrists because of her loneliness over her family being grown and leaving her. Another, Karen, was very young and overwhelmed by having three small children. Sixteen-year-old Tab was down to sixty-seven pounds from anorexia. Manic-depressive Joseph never stopped fantasizing. Nineteen-year-old Ike, just discharged from the Navy, had tried to hang himself. Ryun, a seventeen-year-old, was there because he was a drug addict and couldn't get along with his dad.

One day I got angry with Joseph's endless fantasizing. I said, "Joseph makes me want to throw up. He makes me sick."

"Why, Cynthia?" Mike asked.

Suddenly I had memories of my brother always lying. I saw myself as a scared little girl. Robby was eleven and I saw cigarettes in his pocket and smelled smoke on his breath. I could hear Robby saying, "I didn't steal them, Dad. I didn't smoke." And then I heard the belt and the whops, the cries and screams, and the yelling. The little girl, Cynthia, cried. I was afraid. I was angry at Robby for not telling the truth. If he would tell the truth he wouldn't be spanked. I realized I wasn't really angry at Joseph, but for his reminding me of my brother. These group experiences were making me aware of so many buried emotions that I hated them. I knew God wanted me to look at the truth, but to some extent, ignorance is bliss.

Karen told us she was leaving the hospital because her husband could no longer afford it. He made her many promises if she came home, including her going back to school and getting a job. Someone asked how that was possible if they had no money and she had three children to care for.

"I don't know," she said, "but my husband promised."

I said, "You remind me of a puppet, Karen."

Ike yelled at me, "You are one cold-blooded woman, Cynthia." I couldn't believe his outrage.

Then Karen started yelling at me. "You are so mean, Cynthia. You have no heart. I hate you. I hate it when you are in the room." I was stunned. A few days before, this woman had begged to be my friend.

I thought of all the people in my life who had left me. I looked at the people I was closest to here, and no one defended me except Carrie, who said meekly, "Cynthia isn't cold. She cares."

Mike asked me if Karen reminded me of my mother. "No way," I said. I didn't want to stick around that place, so I went to my room and sobbed into the pillow, "I am no good, no good."

Anna, a new patient, walked into my room and said, "I don't think you're cold, Cynthia. I think you're more perceptive and caring than everyone here." I was touched.

Anna had tried to commit suicide with sleeping pills. She had told the group how her first husband, who had handled all her problems, died suddenly one morning while they were jogging together. Her second husband brought his problems into the marriage, and she longed to have her first husband back.

Later that day, while Anna relived her sorrow with the group, I thought of Matthew, my husband. He had died in a sense, but he was really alive. He took care of me the three years we went together, and then we married. Four months later, he left me all alone. My grief was unbearable. At least Anna's husband had really died. With death, you aren't rejected, but with divorce you are rejected; someone purposely leaves you. I was no good.

Mike looked at me and said, "It's your turn, Cynthia. Come and sit in the chair." I was shaking. "What are you aware of?"

"Grief, loneliness."

"Why?"

"Matthew. Matthew left me, but he didn't die. I wish he did die. I thought he loved me. We spent nearly three years going together, and they were the most wonderful years. Then we married and he left. I was only nineteen years old. It was like he changed overnight. Do you know how humiliating it is to be left?"

Mike said, "That's why you hate men."

"What?"

"Yes, you hate men, Cynthia. Every man in your life has left you: your dad, Robby, Matt, the others, they all left you. You hate men."

The tears poured from my eyes. "I don't, I don't. I just don't trust them."

"Okay," Mike said. "Look at the men in this room and say, 'I trust you.'"

I still shook. I looked at Ike who had told me I was cold. I looked at another man, who bored me. Clint wasn't there. Steven was the only man I could look at and say "I trust you," and at that I hesitated.

Mike told me, "You're to get to know at least eight men while you are here and find out why they don't like you." I sat there stunned. I didn't want to do that. I didn't care if eight men liked me or not. But Mike's eyes told me I'd better do it or else, and I didn't want to find out what the "or else" meant.

9

Tunnel Vision

I had been in the hospital twenty-four days when I got my first pass to go out. I went with Brenda and Steven.

They decided they wanted to go for a nice dinner, so I got all dressed up. It was the first time since being there I had put on makeup and a dress. Everyone said I looked wonderful, but I couldn't readily believe that.

Clint told me I looked gorgeous, which was hard to take, because that day I had become increasingly jealous. Clint was avoiding me and spending more time with Carrie, talking to her the same way he talked to me. When I mentioned it to him, he said, "Well, do something about it." I didn't know what he meant I should do.

We asked Clint to go with us in the evening, but he refused, saying he didn't trust himself. I kept wondering what right I had to want to be with him and to be jealous of Carrie.

Out in the town, my friends and I had a fine time. The food was good at the restaurant we chose, but I couldn't eat much—a real switch. I got up to go to the bathroom and Brenda asked me what I was going to do. I realized she was afraid I was going to throw up. "No, Brenda. I simply have to use the rest room. Don't worry."

We decided to stop at a mall to look around, and it became a frightening experience. While we were walking, my vision suddenly became messed up. The surroundings looked small, the people too close, and it was as though I was going through a moving tunnel. I got dizzy and scared. "Brenda, what is going on? Please take me home. I can't handle this feeling," I cried.

The distorted vision was gone by the time I got back on the ward. A nurse told me it was tunnel vision. "When you go through what you have been going through, the withdrawals and dealing with new feelings, you have what are called psychological blackouts. That's what you had tonight."

"When will I ever be normal?"

"It will take time."

The monster inside me was laughing when I found Clint in the day room talking to Carrie. Clint told me he'd like a life with me but had nothing to offer. I said I needed his strength and friendship. He told me about his moods and looking for dragons at night. Dragons?

"My granddad told me there would be lots of dragons everywhere I went, trying to destroy me. I go crazy sometimes and have to see if I can find them." I didn't know what to say. Clint is scared about his future, and I am scared of Clint.

The next day, Saturday, after Brenda, Elizabeth, and Clint had gone home for the weekend and Clint had been in one of his loser moods, I wrote him a letter telling him he alone could make the decision to change.

I said it with such ease, but what about me? Before he had left he said he would never feel he was good enough for me. But I didn't think I was good enough for him. I had never felt worthy of the love or friendship of any of the men with whom I'd had a relationship, and I always lost them. That was my pattern with men.

That night, my friend Jo, who had once taken me to the doctor, gave me a phone call which upset me. She wanted to know if I had lost weight and if my complexion was clear. She knew I would be gorgeous when I got out of the hospital. There was that old pressure again, that said the only way anyone could accept me was if I were beautiful.

I told a nurse about Jo's call, and she told me I really put the pressure on myself. "After all, didn't your friends know you were always worried about what you ate?"

"Yes, but I tried not to talk about it. Jo knew about my bulimia and that I was dying. But it's like our friendship was based on what I look like."

"Do you have any overweight friends?" the nurse asked.

"No, most of my friends have good bodies. I have one friend who has a big bottom, but she doesn't worry about it and, you know, it has always bothered me. She always seems happy, and I wonder how she can be happy with such a big rear."

The nurse looked at me. "You seem to be not only obsessed with your own body, but with others' as well." She was right. "Do you blame your friend for asking about your body?"

"No, but how can I change this feeling of hating my body?"

"Time, Cynthia," she said. I was beginning to get sick and tired of that time statement.

Sunday morning Dr. Gutierrez allowed me to go to church, my first time in over three weeks. A lady from the church picked me up. It felt fine to get out, but I had to force myself to talk. The poor lady didn't know what to say either, especially when I told her I was in the psychiatric ward.

At church Elizabeth and her family greeted me. Besides having eating disorders in common, we were both Christians. I felt loved by all of them.

A minister I have long admired was the guest speaker. He talked about happiness, and said, "No one person or thing can make me happy. Only I can, and only with God's help." His talk reminded me of a successful heartwarming TV show I produced on people who give, called *Gifts of the Heart*. I did about eleven profiles in all. One man planted a garden for the elderly. He once was bitter about life because he had a heart attack and had to quit the job he loved, but he found that by helping people he became happy. There was another man who became a clown every Saturday and went to the hospitals to entertain the sick children. And there was a rich lady who not only gave her money to good causes, but every day went to the hospital to hold babies, greet sick adults, or write letters. They all had purpose in their lives. They loved people. Thinking about them I wondered if I would ever find my purpose. But for the time being I didn't think I deserved happiness.

After church I introduced myself to the minister. He knew my dad; doesn't everybody? I told him about my death wish and the bulimia. He had never heard of it. I also told him about my news-reporting career. After we talked, I thought about how tired I was of covering murders, car wrecks, fires, and people dying. I remembered the last story I did. A school bus had crashed and nine people were killed, four students and five teachers. I reported the wreck, the funerals, stories of the kids who nearly died, and the pain suffered by all the people connected with it. And I realized I could no longer focus on the world's horrible, cruel events. I wanted to tell good news about people who overcame pain and problems.

Elizabeth's family took me out to eat with them. It was her parents' wedding anniversary. They told about being in college and kissing under an umbrella to avoid getting caught by the strict teachers. You could tell they had a strong committed love. I wondered if that would ever come to me. First, I would have to love myself.

In the evening Robby called from Oregon, where he lives in the woods. We both cried over our pain and emptiness. We loved our parents and wanted them to be proud of us, but we thought we had failed them. Robby told me, "There have been many days I literally put the gun to my head, but my two babies are what helped me to keep going." Robby told me that ever since he was shot in the leg, which left him crippled, he had learned to hold on to one day at a time.

I didn't tell Robby that Mike said I had been trying to be my father's son. Now I realized it was true. Robby was always in trouble,

and for my parents' sake I tried to be what Robby wasn't. After talking
to him, I knew I could not continue doing that.

I sat in the chair and talked to my monster. I had to find out who
the monster was.

"Who are you?" I asked. "What do you want? I hate you, monster."

Mike made me switch chairs, and the monster talked. "You're no
good, Cynthia. You are worthless. You don't deserve to be alive."

I switched chairs. "But I do deserve to be alive, don't I? Who gave
you the right to control me? Who told you to come and destroy me?
Who?" I got in the monster's chair and it stared at me with hatred.
Back in the Cynthia chair I started crying.

Mike said, "When did you become damaged freight, Cynthia?"

"I don't know. All I know is I look in the mirror and hate me. So
many times in the past years, even when I had starved myself for
four days and ran miles and my face looked gaunt, the monster was
laughing at me and saying, 'Just wait; soon your face will be fat. You
don't deserve to be skinny.' I could see my face growing fat."

Mike asked me once again, "When did you become damaged
freight, Cynthia?" I didn't want to know the answer to his question
and he didn't give me the answer, even though I knew that he knew.
He wanted me to come to an awareness of it myself.

In group therapy I talked about Jo's call, Robby's call, and about a
call I also got from my friend, Jessica, whom I worked with at the TV
station. She told me she missed me and that I was her best friend.
That made me feel uncomfortable. She had won some prestigious
awards and I was happy for her but hurt for myself. She was a friend,
yet I felt hurt deep inside me. She had everything: glamour, prestige,
money, marriage. I was her best friend, so why didn't she help me
during the two years I knew her and was dying before her eyes?

Suddenly the glamour and ease of Jessica's life were no longer so
attractive to me.

Mike asked me if I had someone I considered a best friend. "No."

I looked at Clint. He was the only one who understood me, but he didn't know how to be a friend.

Another man in the group, Sam, said, "Cynthia, I feel like you don't need anyone. You give the impression that you are self-sufficient. I wonder why, if you are so self-sufficient, you're in a psychiatric ward."

Tears choked me. "That isn't true. I am so lonely, I feel like I'm dying. But I want to be alive." I knew I had been snobbish toward that older man, avoiding him because the weakness I sensed in him reflected my own insecurity.

Mike said quickly, "Yes, Cynthia, tell us about loneliness."

Something burst inside me, my tears gushed, sobs shook my body. I was so lonely. Pictures were focusing in my mind of that four-year-old little girl, Cynthia, lying in the hospital bed wrapped from her waist down, burning with pain. The hot water had done it. The little girl was crying, and *no one* was there. "Mommy, Daddy, where are you? Where are you?" A nurse came in and yelled at me to grow up and stop crying. But I was hurting with seething pain.

Next to me was a little girl wrapped up like a mummy. The only thing you could see of her were her eyes looking through a maze of bandages. Her mom never came to see her either. "What's wrong? Where are you, Mommy? Daddy?"

I left the group and went to my room. How could I have broken like that in front of those people?

Later, I wanted some security from someone who cared, so I found Clint. But he seemed to be pushing me away, and I asked him why he was acting so distant. What about the letters he had written me? He said he meant what he wrote. "It sounds good on paper, but doing it, living it, is the true test," he said.

I thought, "Yes, but if you really feel good about a friendship you can live it."

Then, with his eyes cold, Clint said, "Oh, Cynthia, you could find someone better than me in the county jail and they would not have done crimes as bad as I have committed."

"I don't care about your past, Clint. If you want to change, you can. Are you telling me to let go of our friendship?"

"Yes. You expect too much. I want to stand alone. I want to be your friend, but I am afraid I will disappoint you."

I told him, "The only thing that will disappoint me is for you to fail yourself, to go back to your old life."

When I crawled into bed, Elizabeth said, "Clint's not good enough for you, Cynthia. I wish you would stay away from him." Wise fourteen-year-old Elizabeth. I wondered if she was right.

10

People Leave

The time was getting closer when Brenda and Clint would be discharged from the hospital. Clint seemed to be retreating from everyone in the group, and when Brenda confronted him about it, he admitted he was scared. We all declared our concern for him. I got sick to my stomach and left, but Mike found me and brought me back to the group.

Mike asked me what was going on. I said that I was upset because Clint and Brenda would be leaving. They had seen me at my ugliest and still cared about me. They had helped me to learn that people, rather than candy bars, fulfilled me.

Mike said, "Say, 'Nothing is forever,' Cynthia."

I couldn't say it.

Back in my room I thought about that, and recalled the people in my life who either left me or I had to leave them: childhood friends, my husband, college friends, boyfriends, friends who got married, friends with babies. My parents were always leaving me, or I them.

People die, move, change, get married, become mothers. Why do they always leave me?

Dear God, please come and grab me. I'm losing these people I have learned to love. Why do you give me people who always leave me? What are you teaching me? I need these people and they need me. Help me cherish them and never forget what they've done for me.

My favorite photographer from the TV station wrote me a letter after I'd been away for a month. He told me all the rumors going around about where I was and what I was doing—I had a nervous breakdown, an ill mother, woman problems, was pregnant—and that everyone was concerned for me. He concluded by saying, "Hurry back. I miss covering the ole murder trials with you. I wish I had some witty gem to end with, but pray to God and eventually he will hear."

We went to the park one day for occupational therapy. It felt good to swing and run and kick a soccer ball. Elizabeth and I walked and talked. She was hoping to go home within a couple weeks, but she was losing weight again. She was also down because she had been remembering friends who rejected her. I told her there would be many rejections in her life: people change and are not perfect. My monster laughed and said, "It's easy to say, Cynthia, but when will you start accepting it?"

Tiny Tab, a sixteen-year-old anorexic who looked like she was seventy, followed me wherever I went. She was a very articulate girl, but always said, "I'm afraid I will tick somebody off." She upset Elizabeth by saying, "If I look like you when I gain my weight, I will feel okay." That devastated Elizabeth. You never talk about bodies or weight or shapes to anorexics. Elizabeth reasoned that, since Tab had to gain weight, Elizabeth herself must be fat by comparison. She was still so concerned about her body, she was not dealing with her more basic problems.

I became the mediator for Tab and Elizabeth. Tab was hurt. She threw her little arms around me and cried with huge sobs, "I'm so lonely, Cynthia. Please be my friend. I need you. We can talk about anything—tea, shoelaces, cars, anything—I don't care. I can't stand to be alone."

I rocked Tab. "I want you too, Tab. I don't want to be alone either."

People in the group were talking about hitting their children, losing their tempers. I shook with fear, and could hear Robby yelling, Dad hitting, and I was the little girl with no place to hide from the screams and agony. I had no one to comfort me.

Mike asked if I was still waiting for my dad to care about me. Between sobs I said, "I look like I have everything together, but I don't. All I want is to share my life with someone, one person to love me and I to love him. That's all I ask."

That night I went to the mall and walked around, but my head pounded, my tunnel vision returned, and my heart was pumping so hard I had to sit down.

I was exhausted when I got up the next morning. Elizabeth stormed in after an overnight pass. She was crying and had been up all night with her mother, upset because she had lost weight and had to stay in the hospital an extra two weeks. I didn't want to hear it because I was grateful to be in the hospital. I didn't want to be, nor dare to be, outside. I told her she was selfish for wanting me to listen to her when she had a mother to comfort her, while I had no one. But that evening we talked it over and forgave each other.

God, it's not going to get better, is it? Life hurts so badly. My feelings are easily hurt. I want to die.

Brenda's last day in the hospital came. I had learned to love her. We had found out her father sexually molested her when she was a child, her mother was mean, she had endlessly cared for younger children and had spent many nights alone in her room crying. But she was so much like me, and understood me. I admired her for conquering her monster, bulimia.

That evening Carrie and I were sitting on the bathroom floor after curfew, talking. She told me Clint was backing away from me because I was expecting more of our friendship than was there. Clint was now interested in Carrie, and she in him. So, Clint turned out to be a liar. What was there about me that caused this to happen?

I started laughing, and it scared Carrie. "Why are you laughing?"

"Oh, I am glad this happened. I am so embarrassed that I fell for his lies. I do this every time with guys. I always fall for the guys I know won't stay." I laughed some more at my stupidity.

When I got in bed I was sad, but I had more of a sense of relief. Yet, there was the thought that I have this pattern with men.

In group therapy I learned that, for some odd reason, I was special. I was telling Anna that if she was really angry she had to sound angry, and suddenly the focus was on me.

Tab said she admired me for not being afraid of saying what was on my mind. Anna said, "I wish people would respond to me like they do to Cynthia." Mike got a look in his eyes and made Anna and me switch seats and roles. It was hilarious. Quaint, feminine Anna raised her arms and put her legs out, gesturing how she felt. She became, through body language, me. I hadn't realized I was so expressive with my body.

Ike said, "I am really envious of you, Cynthia. You are so friendly and open and honest, and you're not afraid to say how you feel." This was the same man who had said I was cold-blooded?

Then Candy said, "You're unique, Cynthia. You let people know where they stand with you, and I know you care about them."

I left the group that day feeling okay. Okay? That was a new feeling.

In my individual therapy session Mike told me to remember anything I wanted—memories, pictures from the past. I saw a pretty white church made of wood. I was a toddler and someone was holding me. I was looking at the church in front of which my dad was shaking hands and hugging people. I wanted him to notice me, thinking, "Daddy, why aren't you holding me? Why are you touching everyone else and not me?" But he didn't look at me.

It seemed so real I had to call my mother. "What did the church look like when I was a toddler? What color was it?"

"It was white."

"What was it made of?"

"Wood."

I started sobbing into the phone. "Oh, Mom, even as a toddler I was lonely. Did you want me? Dad and you didn't want me, did you?"

"Oh, Cynthia, Dad and I wanted you so much. You were planned, and you only brought joy to our lives."

"Really, Mom? But I was so lonely."

One day Mike lectured about people who search for the great mother, the one person who will be everything to them. The problem is that no one is indispensable nor perfect; no one human being can be everything to us. I knew I only sought out people I thought could fulfill me, and ignored the rest. Was that what Tye meant when he said I associated only with a few certain people?

Mike went on to say that most people who come to the psychiatric ward are seeking the great mother. They have become isolated and disillusioned because their best friends or mates or parents can't possibly be everything to them. Instead, we all need God and many people in our lives. Each friend can meet specific needs.

I thought about that. There were very few people who filled me. I didn't want just a drop from someone, I wanted a cupful from the people in my life. Was I wrong to feel that way? Was that a reason I became so sick? As I looked back, I had no one in my life when I left my TV job, except maybe one girlfriend, but no one who understood me. Why?

It struck me that somehow I always got attached to people who didn't give much of anything I wanted in return, and I made all the people who cared about me go away. When ever someone like Fred, a widower whom I sometimes took out to eat, told me I was sweet to him, I didn't believe him. I didn't think I deserved to be called a good person.

But God, I am not worthless. You tell me in your word that I'm significant to you, that you think about me so many times each day that I can't even count them (Psalm 139). Why can't I believe you? Does my disbelief really stem from my childhood, as the doctors here imply? Please help me to become aware of the truth, Lord, even if it hurts.

Around this time, Carrie, Elizabeth, and I were talking about the possibility of my writing a book. I was beginning to want to tell others about what I was learning about myself and bulimia. I was starting to realize that the bulimia, my monster, was an addiction, just like alcoholism or drug addiction. My two friends thought I should do it. It seemed right to me, too.

The day before Clint was to leave, he was afraid. He said his wife wanted him to remain an alcoholic. He told the group that all the men in her life were animals who abused her. She must have a need for animals, and now, suddenly, Clint wasn't a mean animal, and his wife couldn't handle it. Mike told Clint, "I wonder if you can handle your wife."

"I don't know if I want to."

"I wonder if you can accept her love for you, Clint."

Clint said, "I don't think she knows how to love."

I asked Clint, "Do you, Clint? Do you know how to love?"

"I don't know, Cynthia. I just don't know."

The next day, when Clint was leaving, I gave him a letter in which

I encouraged him and told him to remember us when he needed help getting through his scary life. Then we held each other, cried, thanked each other, and I told him I would never say good-bye. I didn't know then how valuable my experience with Clint had been to me.

11

Divorce

My first overnight pass from the hospital was for a visit with Brenda. It was my thirty-seventh day as a patient, a Friday.

My head started to pound before I left, but one of the nurses said, "Enjoy yourself. Smell the world. See it and enjoy it."

Walking to my car, I wondered if I would overeat and want the pink pills. When I began driving I thought about being discharged from the hospital. Would I go back to reporting, or would I write a book? Was I crazy to consider that drastic change? I was at peace when I thought about the book, and in turmoil when I thought about going back to car wrecks, murders, and rapes.

Away from Dallas's high buildings the countryside became beautifully green and hilly. I rolled down the window and felt the rain on my arm and face. It felt good and smelled good to be savoring God's world.

Brenda fixed a great dinner. It was good to be with her. After dinner we took a long walk around her property. She and her husband, who was away on a plane trip, owned thirty acres, with sheep, cows, dogs, kittens, and a large garden. Brenda talked about love for her husband and her fear he might leave. The day before, she had nearly regressed. She thought she had overeaten, and, being alone, had to fight her desire to purge; but, instead, she took a walk.

"Oh, Brenda, at least you didn't do it. You did something constructive for yourself. When will we stop being so obsessed with our bodies?"

During the night my dreams were of Clint, Brenda, food, Mom and Dad, struggle. The thunder awakened me and I was moaning. The next morning my face was swollen; I was ugly and unlovable. But Brenda's daughter made me feel lovable. She shared her dolls with me, made me a paper flower, and hugged me. A child made me feel loved. I left Brenda's house thinking I had to get back to the hospital and share that kind of childlike love, with no conditions asked nor expected.

That evening Steven and I went to town to a Ben Vereen concert. I wore my "lollipop" dress, and Steven said I looked stunning. Steven looked smashing, too, wearing a suit. His color was returning to his face. We had to stop at the store to buy him a tie.

For a few hours we felt good and talked about how glad we were to be alive. Steven told me about his drug addiction, how the LSD and heroin made everything seem better—work, sex, play. But then he became paranoid and realized he was going insane. He was glad to be rehabilitated. He found God, but he became so intense and so analytical about the relationship, he got legalistic with God and ended up feeling empty.

Two weeks before coming to the hospital, he planned to blow his brains out. But someone, without his knowing, had borrowed his firearm. He prayed to God, and that very day a friend told Steven about the Minirth-Meier Clinic and gave him the money to go for help.

Two weeks before I came to the hospital, I, too, envisioned a gun to my head. I asked God to kill me. As Steven and I talked we took each other's hands and squeezed tightly. We were grateful to be alive and to have each other. We were learning to feel again, even though it was mostly pain at that point.

Oh, God, thank you for not allowing Steven to take his life, and thank you for saving mine, too.

Ben Vereen was fantastic. I will never forget his song about colors. He sang, "Don't give me black sadness, give me colors of life," while he did a routine with brightly-colored scarves. I thought to myself, "One of these days my life will be hot pinks and reds and lovely purples, not black." I had always worn black or brown, colors that hid my body.

On the way home I told Steven about Clint and what had happened. Steven said, "I'm sure Clint cares about you, but I really hope he gives his wife a chance. If he can give her love, maybe she can grasp it."

Steven told me he himself had given up on his first wife. She loved him but he couldn't believe anyone could love him, so he ran away even though he loved her.

That night, in contrast to most of my nights, I had no nightmares and didn't sleep fretfully; I simply slept.

The sermon in church the next day was from Isaiah, about the clay and the potter, and I began to think about God's plan for our lives.

God, I know you're there, and I'm beginning to listen to you. You are the one to shape my life. But too often I think I am the potter and I will mold my own life. That's what I've been doing, but now I'm tired of my reporting job and the things I was reporting. God, mold me, and help me to tell people about your goodness. I am listening to you.

My cousin Diana and her husband Mark came to have lunch with me, and thought I looked well. Mark said there had always been a shell around me, ever since he met me during my senior year in high school, when the bulimia began, and that he never knew how to break through it. I said I loved being with them because they made me happy, and whenever we had to leave each other I had to be tough about saying good-bye. Mike's voice echoed in my mind, "Nothing is forever."

I told them more about my addiction, how I spent up to $300 a week on food and laxatives. Mark was amazed, and said that explained why I was always broke, even though he knew I made good money.

One story I told them was from my college days, when I didn't have much money so sometimes stole food. I never thought of it as stealing, but the monster attacked me while I was grocery shopping. One time I opened a jar of peanuts and ate them in the aisle. Before that I opened a package of wieners, ate three, then put the package back on the shelf, as I did the empty peanuts jar. An undercover policeman approached me and said, "Lady, I saw what you did."

I looked straight at him and said, "What are you talking about?"

"I saw you open the jar of peanuts and eat them. That's called shoplifting."

I lied about what he accused me of doing, and in the back of my mind was saying, "Yeah, and what about the wieners?"

"I ought to arrest you right now," he told me, "but this is a warning. If you ever do this again, I will put you in jail."

I realized as I left the store, shaking, that I was sick. I never stole food again, but spent a lot of money, so that even though I earned much, I had little to show for it.

Back at the hospital I told the other bulimics the story. They said they used to go into stores and eat huge bags of candy; they were never caught, and all of them somehow justified what they were doing.

The occupational therapist was going over drawings I had done, and I was learning some things about myself I didn't like and didn't want to believe. "For your age, profession, and maturity," she said, "these pictures are extremely childish."

"Well, I'm not an artist."

"No, that has nothing to do with it. You've got a little girl locked inside, Cynthia. Here's a picture you drew of a baby. What were you thinking?"

"Someday I want to have a baby."

"No, Cynthia. This baby is angry. You painted its head red; red means anger. And the expression on its face is angry. What is this picture about?"

"You asked me where I was in my life. I drew a big mountain with me climbing it. I am always climbing it. I am always climbing hard and never making it to the top."

"Now look at you in the picture," she said. "Look at the stick girl. All your shapes are like a male."

"What? Come on, Marta, give me a break." I was beginning to get embarrassed.

"Take a look," she said. "In every picture you've drawn, all the shapes are like a male."

I was angry. "So tell me, Miss Freud, what does this mean?"

"Mike says it means you're trying to be the son and the daughter of your family."

I went to see Mike. "What does it mean, that I am my father's son?" I demanded.

"Just that," he said. "You are the son and daughter of your family. Robby was never the son your dad wanted him to be. He doesn't have the prestigious job nor the personality your dad wanted him to have, and he's not the athlete your dad was. So you chose to make your dad happy by saying, 'If Robby won't do it, then I will.'"

"I don't believe you, Mike." I started crying. "Does that explain why I haven't felt feminine for years?"

"Well, I have noticed your clothes are very businesslike. You wear only suits if you go out of the hospital, and in the hospital you wear long shirts that cover you. You're the son and daughter of your family."

My tears were of bitter anger.

Before I went to bed I ate a bunch of cookies and popcorn. My stomach was full, but I punished myself. I was sick and hated myself for eating, then wanted to get rid of the food. I ate sneakily, because everyone was in the day room. I was okay one minute, then I ate, and my whole disposition changed. Steven noticed. "What's wrong, Cynthia?"

"I don't know. Leave me alone." I went to bed.

My sleep was disturbed by nightmares of people and loneliness. During the night my husband, Matthew, came into the picture. One cold October morning, shortly after we were married, he came home at 2 A.M. He crawled into bed with me and seemed like a stranger. I said, "Matthew, why are you treating me so badly? Why don't you come home at night? Why won't you touch me? I feel like you don't love me."

His back was toward me. He turned to me with cold, hateful eyes. "I don't love you. I've never loved you and I want you *out of my life!*" The man I loved, with whom I had spent two and a half years, my husband, was rejecting me! I shook with sobs and became nauseated. Suddenly I was back in my hospital bed.

Elizabeth woke up and said, "What's wrong, Cynthia?"

"Oh, Elizabeth, I feel so alone." I had visions of blowing my brains out. "I want to die."

Jay, an aide, came and took me to the day room. I told him about Matthew and Clint. "There is some connection, Jay. I have a pattern with men. Here are two totally different men, yet they both do the same things with their wives. Why do I do this to myself? I'm afraid I will marry someone and cry in the night, and he won't comfort me, but will reject me."

"What kind of a man do you want, Cynthia?" Jay asked.

"Someone who cares, who will listen to me and help me feel loved."

"What about a true Christian man? Why haven't you mentioned that quality? If you marry a committed Christian, he'll know how to comfort and love you because, if he's committed to God, he'll know how to be committed to you."

"Maybe. But I don't feel worthy. My husband was a 'Christian,' but he left me. Now, many Christian guys have ignored me, because they are afraid of the stigma of my being a divorcee. Jay, I want to be committed to God, and worthy of a Christian's love. What do I do?"

"Begin by reading the Bible. Savor it, dwell on it, believe it, practice it," Jay said.

As I crawled back into bed, I heard Mike's question, "When did you become damaged freight, Cynthia?"

At 7:30 A.M. Mike was knocking on my door. He motioned me to follow him into a secluded room. "Start talking," he said.

"Mike, why was I attracted to Clint? He is cruel. I'm always attracted to those who need a social worker. I've never felt good enough to be with someone who was 'good,' someone who had no problems. Matthew and I dated for two years. Two months before the wedding I knew something wasn't right. But when I tried to call off our wedding, Matthew cried and said he couldn't live without me. His parents pressured me by saying, 'But, Cynthia, the invitations are out, and the showers. You can't back out now. You two love each other.' I loved Matthew so I married him. But after three months, it was over. He said he'd never loved me. Why did he marry me?"

"Hmm, neither one of you wanted to get married, yet you married each other." Mike paused. I hated it when he paused; I knew he was going to hurt me. "Your husband didn't leave you, Cynthia. He was tired of *therapy*."

That rang a bell. It was true; I was always lifting up Matthew. He made bad grades and I said, "Come on, Matthew, you can do it." His dad wanted him to be a pro baseball player, but he never came up to it. I encouraged him to do better. Matthew had potential and I was going to be the one to make his world wonderful.

Bluntly, Mike said, "In a manner of speaking, you were married to your brother. That's why every man you are attracted to needs help. You've tried to save your whole family. You're Robby's savior and your dad's son. You're stuck, Cynthia."

"But, Mike, how do I overcome all that?" I cried. "How do I not fall for men who have problems or haven't quite made it?"

Matthew still hadn't done anything with his life. After we divorced he married a young girl he had gotten pregnant while we were married. Now he's on his third marriage, with two children.

There had been numerous other men in my life also, but no one I really cared about, and if I did care, I knew I couldn't marry them. William, who was an agnostic, came from a poor family but he had potential. Then there was Clint. "Mike, why was I attracted to Clint?"

Mike sarcastically said, "Clint was beaten, Robby was beaten. You're attracted to men like your brother. Since Mom and Dad couldn't handle or help Robby, you are covering up your pain and guilt for him by getting involved with the Robbys of the world."

"You're right. What do I do to change?"

"Well, if you want a good man, you ask the guy before you go on a date, 'Have you been beaten?' If he says yes, you run as fast as you can the other way."

After Mike told me why I hadn't looked for the right kind of man, I ate two chocolate eclairs from the dinner trays and made myself sick. I was punishing myself again. I didn't deserve to feel good.

God, please change these feelings. Help me understand. Help me not to be a therapist to men. I want to share my life with someone, but I want the right one.

I went to my room. Visions of my brain splattered against the hospital room wall came to my mind. I couldn't handle the reasons for my self-destruction, confusion, and frustration. I was stuck. I wanted to get out of the mess and really start living. I went back to the day room and ate two more eclairs and some cookies. Why face myself? It was too painful.

Tab was watching me. I could tell she wanted me to stop eating but was afraid to tell me. She finally said, "How was your session with Mike?"

"Awful."

"Is that why you're eating the eclairs?"

"Yes."

"Why don't you talk, Cynthia?"

"Because I want to destroy myself, Tab, so leave me alone."

Back in my room again, I cried into my pillow, "Oh, Robby, Robby, you always thought I didn't love you, but I've been longing to help you all these years."

While I was thinking, there was a knock on my door. It was the lady from the insurance office to tell me my insurance would be up in four days and I'd have to pay the $600 a week myself. If I couldn't pay cash, I'd have to leave. I had thought my insurance would pay for all my time there. Panic set in and I called Mom.

"I'm so sick, Mom. If I leave now, I will die. I won't make it. I went shopping this week and I didn't feel normal. My parts aren't together. Mom, what do I do?"

"Cynthia, don't worry about the money. Dad and I will find a way. You just get well. Concentrate on nothing else. You stay there as long as it takes."

"Mom, I'm sorry I'm sick. I don't want to die."

"I love you, Cyndi. Please get well."

"Mom, I love you."

12

Rape

In occupational therapy the next day, I worked with clay. Marta gave me a big blob of brown clay, and I ripped it to pieces and threw it. My arms hurt, I threw it so hard. "Is that how you see your life, Cynthia? Look at the way you have beaten the clay and taken it apart."

"Yes, I feel my life is all in pieces, like the hearts. Nothing connects."

"Okay, make something with the clay," Marta said. I formed a cup. Its handle was broken. "Why a cup, Cynthia?"

"Because I need to be filled up by something or someone." I was tense.

After occupational therapy, the mail came. I got forty letters that day! One patient said, "And you aren't loved?" Letters, cards, words from people who loved me. Dad wrote and told me not to worry about money. He just wanted me to get well. He said he loved me more than life. He told me to read Psalm 147. I opened the Bible to the passage:

> (The Lord) heals the brokenhearted
> and binds up their wounds,
> He determines the number of the stars
> and calls them each by name.
> Great is our Lord and mighty in power,
> His understanding has no limit.

Carrie's story came out in group therapy. When she was about twelve her dad was telling her she was no good. When she was fourteen the unthinkable happened. Her best friend of over two years took her out one night. They were both drinking, but he encouraged her to drink more. She got drunk, and the next thing she knew, her friend drove her to a woods, pulled her out of his car onto the ground, ripped her clothes off and raped her. Raped her! He was her best friend, and she wondered what she did to cause him to rape her.

When she got home with ripped clothes, blood on her face from where her friend had hit her during her struggle, her dad just looked at her without a word, as if she deserved what happened. She never told anyone else until that day in therapy, five years after it happened.

"You suffered violence. That horrible guy had no right to do what he did. Why didn't you tell someone, Carrie?"

"I always thought it was all my fault."

"Carrie, you have got to get mad. You *have* to get angry."

"I can't, Cynthia. It had to be my fault."

Mike shot out, "Maybe we ought to just hit Carrie, and then she'd be accepted. She wants us to hit her around, give her some verbal abuse and then maybe she can trust us."

"Stop it, Mike," Carrie said. But the look on her face told me she thought that was what she deserved. She then said that her dad used to beat her when she was bad. Once he threw a hibachi at her. Another time she was in a swimsuit, and he chased her with a pool stick and hit her. She had bruises all over her legs.

"But what did you do to deserve that?"

"I don't remember, but I must have been bad. I am bad. My dad has always told me I am bad."

"You aren't bad, you aren't," I cried. "You are sweet and beautiful and sensitive. You aren't bad. It's your dad who's bad. I don't like your dad, Carrie."

Everyone in the room told Carrie that they loved her and that she didn't deserve all that emotional pain. "Carrie, you're good."

But Carrie hung her head down. I knew she didn't hear us, or if she did, she didn't believe us.

I was angry at her and didn't know what to do. My anger churned deep inside. I could hear the monster rattling its chains.

Carrie talked about her rape a number of times after that, and each time she did, I agonized. It chilled my bones and made me shudder. Why? Was it simply because I cared about Carrie, or was it something else? I'd never been raped, and the thought made me sick. Something was deeply wrong, but what was it? It seemed the monster was laughing.

The nurse asked me to talk to a new patient, Lindy. Lindy was bulimic as well as diabetic. When I walked into her room, she was lying on her bed and her eyes were swollen from crying. She was thirty-two years old and had a husband and two children. For fifteen years she had binged and purged. Lindy, like me, started in college as a way to control her weight. She, too, felt a tremendous pressure to be the perfect daughter.

I revealed some of the truths about myself that I had learned in the hospital. Lindy understood. She had an older brother who was rebellious. She also had a baby sister, making Lindy the middle child, and no one paid much attention to her, so she took control by binging and purging. Her dad had died when she was ten.

We talked about our frustrations with doctors: asking for help because we were so desperate and finding most of them didn't know what bulimia was nor what to do. "Would you believe, Lindy, the last doctor I went to see said a man would be the answer! Every time I left him I bought ten candy bars, and yet I kept seeing him because I was so desperate."

Lindy had an insulin reaction before being admitted. That morning at 4 A.M. she had baked two cakes, ate them and threw up. Then she shot a double dose of insulin. She was very sick and could have died. I hoped I could help Lindy in some way.

The next day was "day out" for the patients, and they decided to go bowling. I wasn't planning to go, but the rest wanted me to. Ike came and told me that everyone wanted me to bum with them. Me? You want to be with me, you guys? It felt good to be wanted. I had fun but got exhausted.

When we got back, I went to say hello to Lindy, but she was out of her room. The nurse told me she was in intensive care because of an insulin reaction following her double dose of insulin after the cake binge, purge, and not eating for a day.

In the evening Steven and I went for a walk. My dear friend Steven; I got much comfort from him. He talked to me and listened without being overly analytical.

He wanted to know what my addiction was all about. I told him about all the food and laxatives, that I was an over-the-counter drug addict.

"My brother always thought I was Goody Two-shoes, and I'm a drug addict. I'm suffering from withdrawals. Steven, do you suppose one reason I started it was to prove to Robby that I'm not perfect?"

"It makes sense."

A memory came to my mind.

"A year ago, I was in a car wreck. I had binged all day. It had been a week since William left me. I was so empty. At work I ate and ate. There were so many stories to do that day I was never free to go to the bathroom to throw up, and I didn't have any laxatives with me. So right after work, I rushed out. It was raining. I got on the freeway in a mad dash to the store for my pills. I wasn't watching, I was in such a hurry. A truck stopped in front of me and I looked behind me to pass him. My car crashed into that truck and my face was smashed into the steering wheel. It knocked a hole in my chin. I had sixty stitches, and as the doctor was sewing me up, I wasn't concerned about the scar on my television face; I was more concerned about the food in my stomach. I was so afraid of getting fat. Do you know, it was about six months before my mouth was normal, and to this day, my smile is crooked. I had that wreck because of my addiction. I could have been maimed or ruined for life." I shook as I recalled the car accident. Steven held me, and it felt good to be hugged.

Carrie told me something I will never forget, because I cared deeply about her well-being. She said that she kept having a dream in which she was struggling for breath. While she was in bed an attacker hit her, and she was afraid of dying. I walked into the dream and saw that she couldn't breathe, so I comforted her. I hugged her, and suddenly she could breathe.

In group therapy we figured out what the dream meant. Mike made Carrie close her eyes and relax. What she remembered happened when she was about four. She had a severe case of asthma, and in order to open her breathing passage, her parents would put her on a wooden ledge over the bathtub. In the tub was boiling hot water. Little Carrie cried and screamed for fear she would fall into that water. Her mom and dad would hold her down and tell her to be quiet. The parents, too, were probably worried, and in their panic were rough on her and yelled at her. That was the source of the fearsome dream.

I was terrified as Carrie talked and cried tears of anguish. I thought it was because of Carrie's pain that I was in such pain. But Mike knew otherwise. "What are you thinking of, Cynthia?"

"Why did her parents do that? Didn't they know she was scared?"

"Why are you so angry, Cynthia? Close your eyes. What are you aware of?"

No, no, no. Memories flooded my eyes. I didn't want to think about them, but they came anyway. There I was again, the poor little four-year-old girl, burned from my waist down, all wrapped up in bandages. I was sleeping. The lights were out in my hospital room.

Suddenly the door opened and the light was turned on. There were three big men in white outfits and three big women in white outfits. They pulled me from my side, opened my legs, and started tearing away the outer layers of my burned skin. "Oh, please, please, I'll be good. Please, please, I promise I will be good." But they kept on. They kept on poking and grabbing and pulling at that place. Nobody had ever touched me there. I knew they weren't supposed to. "Please stop. I'll go to sleep. I'll be a good girl. Please go away."

One of the nurses turned to me and said, "Well, then, go to sleep and shut up."

"Oh, Mommy, Daddy, where are you? Where are you? Don't you love me? What are these people doing to me? Why are they hurting me? I've been trying to be good. Where are you, Mom? Where are you, Dad?"

I opened my eyes. The group was staring at me. Carrie was sobbing. I was drained, and still sobbed; I had cried so hard I couldn't catch my breath. Mike looked at me hard. "It's like you've been raped, isn't it, Cynthia? They did something to you which you knew was wrong."

"Yes, yes. Why did they do that?" There was a nurse in our group. I looked at her angrily and asked, "Why did they do that to a little four-year-old girl? Were they getting their kicks?"

The nurse said that it was probably for preventive measures. I may have had a staph infection, and they were actually protecting me.

"But why did they not tell me that? Who did that nurse think she was? I was only four years old, only a little girl."

"Those were the dark ages, Cynthia. They didn't allow visitors in the burn unit, or you may have been in isolation. They were treating you the best they knew how. But they didn't know about kids' emotions. Call it ignorance."

Mike asked, "When did you become damaged freight, Cynthia?" My body shook with grief. The whole roomful of people seemed to be shocked. I had my hands wrapped around me, and Carrie had her arms around her knees. I was rocking, and Carrie was staring into midair. "What did you want, Carrie and Cynthia, when you experienced those events?" Mike asked.

"I wanted my mom and dad to hold me. Carrie wanted the same from her mom and dad."

Mike's voice boomed out, "Well, Mommy and Daddy aren't here, but you two are here. What are you waiting for? Reach out to each other."

I took the first step, and Carrie and I fell into each other's arms. We wrapped our pain and sorrow and hate around each other, and all those deep secrets lifted. We gave each other the warmth and love and comfort that those horrid parents and nurses and doctors never gave us when we were only four years old.

Now I knew that the moment I'd decided I was damaged freight was when I was severely burned accidently at age four. And I finally realized why Mike had been gently and patiently asking me for weeks, "Cynthia, when did you become damaged freight in your own eyes?"

It finally clicked.

13

Mom and Dad

My forty-fourth day in the hospital Mom and Dad came for the first time. It was for our family therapy. I didn't want to see them, nor to have them see me ugly and disconnected. All morning I was a nervous wreck, embarrassed and ashamed, afraid I would hurt them.

Dealing with family dynamics is an important segment of the Minirth-Meier therapy program. Following weeks of group and individual therapy, I began to see that my place in my family's organization, with our personal interactions, had been a major part of my development into the person I was. Certainly, I had problems that, in part at least, originated in our family's problems, and that had likely generated and reinforced my eating problems.

Family therapy is an opportunity for the patient and her family members together to further explore and assess their relationships, as well as to get help in understanding her problem and information as to how to support her progress. The therapist helps the family to alter the relationships that are

> destructive to the patient, thereby resolving their old prob-
> lems and developing new, more positive patterns. Fre-
> quently, this includes guiding the patient to break her
> destructive emotional ties to her family.

Mike told me my parents were in the waiting room. I went through the locked doors of the psychiatric wards and my body seemed numb. I turned the corner into the waiting room and saw Dad's shoes, then their faces. My tears started pouring and the sobs came. Then I felt the two people who gave me life embrace me. I heard sobs and pain, and the sounds weren't coming only out of my mouth. Then we went into the group therapy room.

As we sat there, Dad on my left, Mom on my right, and Mike facing us, I folded my arms. Mike said, "What are you doing, Cynthia?"

"I don't know. It feels secure, I guess."

"Why don't you reach out?"

"Because it's so hard, Mike."

"Go ahead, Cynthia, reach out."

It was difficult, but I put out my hands to my mother and father. They immediately grasped my hands, and I broke down. My pain was so intense, I went into my dad's arms and sobbed. I embraced Mom and she told me she loved me. We were all blowing our noses. Mike just happened to have a big box of tissues.

"So, what do you want to talk about, Cynthia?" Mike said.

"I don't know."

"Huh? Why don't you tell them about feeling responsible for your whole family."

"I do, Mom and Dad. I have been dying for our family. I have felt pressure to save our family, whether you intended for me to do it or not." Suddenly, my anger surfaced. "And where were you when I needed you? Dad, you always, always put the church and that college, and other people before us, before me. When I won Miss Teenage Christian and got a scholarship for college and a trip to Europe, I didn't win it for me; I won it for you and Mom. Yet, the very first thing you said to me when I got home from the pageant was, 'Just because you won this, Cynthia, don't get a big head.' So what? So what? Why didn't you hug me and tell me how proud you were of me? Why wasn't I ever good enough for you, Dad?"

Dad said, "I'm sorry, I didn't know I made you feel that way. When you won Miss Teenage Christian, that was the proudest moment of my life."

"Then why, why didn't you tell me?"

Mike asked my dad a question. "What did the church you preached in look like when Cynthia was a baby?"

"Well," Dad said, "it was white, made of wood, with a forest surrounding it."

I understood what Mike was getting at. His question was about my memories of a couple of weeks ago. He was trying to find out if they were true events locked in my subconscious.

I asked my mom, "Why didn't you and Dad want me?"

"But we did, Cynthia. You were planned. We wanted you desperately."

"Then why did I feel that way, even as a child?"

"Perception, Cynthia," Mike said. "You decided as a young toddler that you didn't want to bother anyone."

"But we were always there, Cynthia." Mom said.

"So why didn't I feel that?"

Mom said, "Probably because we were always running after Robby."

My anger rose again. "Robby, Robby, Robby! That's all I heard all my life. Robby this, Robby that. What about me? Your attention was always on Robby. I'll bet, Dad, that you never talked about me to anyone, did you? You never talked about your daughter. It was always Robby, your son."

"Probably that's so because there was no need to worry about you. You were the perfect child."

"Yeah, the perfect child who now hates life and wants to die. Thank you very much, Mom and Dad."

Dad said sadly, "You were a child that did not seem to need anyone. Robby loved to sleep with us and hug us. You always wanted to sleep in your own bed. I remember putting you to bed and you just giggled as I said good night."

"Even then I never wanted to bother anyone."

"We made a lot of mistakes," Dad admitted. "Do you remember all the people that lived with us while you were growing up? Your mom and I realize now that we should never have done that. We were always keeping college kids, having guests. We expected you to be perfect, and you were."

"I hate being perfect. There is such pressure to be perfect."

Dad continued, "As far as knowing you were sick, I realized it the last time you were home." He looked at Mike, "She has always been so loving and friendly. That time she was hostile. No matter what we said, she was angry. We went to church that Sunday, and she got up and left the service. We found her in the car. Everyone was asking about her, because everyone wanted to see her. She was always so people oriented, but that day I knew something was seriously wrong. That was not my Cyndi."

"I remember that Sunday. I went home to tell my parents I was losing my sanity. I couldn't work, I couldn't write, I couldn't talk to anyone. I didn't know how. I was there to tell them I could not handle life any more. But I didn't, I couldn't tell them I was dying. When I left them that weekend, my thoughts were filled with killing myself. I stopped at every store along the 350 miles and ate and threw up and took pills."

"Why didn't you tell us how desperate you were, Cynthia?"

"Because you wouldn't have believed me. After all, a year before I told you what I was doing—that I was up to sixty pills a day—and you told me that I did not do that."

"I thought you were just daring me," Dad said. "I had no idea; and yet, I guess it was my own denial that my perfect daughter was sick."

"Okay, Cynthia," Mike said, "Close your eyes and let's go back to four years old."

I hugged myself and the tears fell. I cried out, "Oh, the hot water, the pain." I saw myself running, then alone in the hospital. "Why weren't you there? Why did you leave me? Why, why, why?" I opened my eyes. "Where were you?"

"We were there, Cynthia," Mom said. "I was out in the waiting room the whole time. Daddy was on the road when you were burned, but he came as soon as he could. We spent night and day in the waiting room."

"Why didn't someone tell me that? Why, why, why?"

Memories came to Mom. "The doctor let you go home, even before you should have. Do you remember that?"

"No."

"We wanted to be there with you. Do you remember that our doctor came every day to bathe your burns?"

"No, I don't remember." I started sobbing again. "If you were there, why don't I remember? Why didn't someone tell me?"

"It's a child's perception, Cynthia," Mike said. "So when did you become damaged freight? You see, your isolation, your feelings of no one caring about you began way before your burns, but your burns added to those feelings. The child only knew pain. You blocked out the good things that happened to you because your subconscious wouldn't allow you to remember them. So, as you have grown up, you have protected yourself from getting hurt, because after all, if Mom and Dad aren't there when you're in pain, who will be?"

Dad hugged me with his strong arms. "I always wanted to hug you, but you would never let me."

"I didn't want to bother you. You were always too busy." I cried into his arms. I felt a sense of relief. My parents had never left me; they were always there. But no one had told that scared little girl.

Dr. Gutierrez gave me an overnight pass to be with Mom and Dad. I wasn't too sure if I really wanted to go, but Mike seemed to think it was important. We went out to eat, we talked, we even laughed. My Dad was very good at telling jokes, but I could never remember them. Could it be I figured I could never tell them as well as he did, so why try to remember?

We played rummy that night. Something happened that often occurred in my family. Somehow I was bending the cards, and Dad commented, "Don't bend the cards." Then Mom almost got some pop on her cards, and Dad said gruffly, "Joye, don't ruin the cards."

I started to yell with newly-found glee, "Oh, no, no! The cards, these precious cards, may get ruined. Oh, my, what will we do? My friends are all dying in the hospital, but Daddy, these wonderful playing cards may get ruined, and I'm afraid the whole world will end. Oh, what will we do?"

My dad, mom, and I broke into uncontrollable laughter. The point was made. I realized how I used to worry over burned toast, or that my clothes were never pretty enough—always frivolous, ridiculous worries about unimportant things.

That evening we all learned something important about our priorities and how they affected us.

14

Not Damaged Freight

We had another family therapy session the next day. I had told Mike I saw over fifteen doctors, therapists, psychiatrists, and other professionals over the last nine years seeking help. Some of them just looked at me and said, "You do what? Well then, stop it!" Or, I would get the old statement to "believe in God and everything will be all right." The last doctor I saw said, "What you need is a man. That will solve all your problems. Find a man and you'll be cured." I was angry at those so-called professionals.

Mike wondered why none could help me. "Did you really tell them how desperate you were?"

"I thought I did. I was honest about all I was doing to my body."

"But did you tell them you were thinking about putting a gun to your head?"

"No, I don't think so."

"How can anyone really help you unless you are totally honest with them?" Mike said.

Then the subject changed to men. Did we really have to talk about men in front of my parents? Mike looked at them and said, "You know, I think it's really sad. Many Christian women say they don't want to have a home. But women like Cynthia are so busy saving their families they never have a real life of their own. There are a lot of fears about marriage, fears about breaking away from Mom and Dad."

I started crying, "I'm afraid that you two will die and leave me, and I will have no one. You are the only people I have, my only family connection, my security. The thought of your dying hurts and angers me, too. I was angry when you didn't acknowledge I was sick. But I'm angry, too, that you are the only two people on this earth I have to depend on and who love me."

"But why is it that way?" Mike said. "Why did you give up on other people? When did you become damaged freight?"

"Oh, the pain of those doctors 'raping' me. Where, where were you, Mom and Dad?" I relived once again being the little girl sleeping, the light coming on, the three men and three women opening my legs and pulling at my skin. My parents were shocked. They never knew that had happened.

Then I said angrily, "And all my life you have been worried about my scars. While growing up, you said maybe I needed plastic surgery, I might not get married, the scars would affect the man who wanted to marry me; messages that always said, 'You're not good enough.'"

Dad started talking, "First of all, Cynthia, I plan on living till I'm 100 years old. You don't have to worry about your Mom's and my dying for a long time. Secondly, we were concerned about your burns. We didn't want you to be hurt by those scars. We never intended to make you feel you weren't good enough. We were only worried that *you* might feel inferior with your scars. We didn't know any better. Please forgive us."

Mike also told my parents that I was trying to save the family, and, most of all, to be Robby's savior. Flashes of my running out of the house when Robby got into trouble came to my mind. "You two never came to me whenever you beat Robby. You never came into my room. You may not know this, but when all the crying and whipping went on, I would run out of the house and hide behind the tree in our back yard, because the sounds frightened me so badly. Yet nobody knew I was hurting." My sobs were becoming unbearable.

"Your daughter, in a sense, married your son, Mr. and Mrs. Rowland. She has been looking for Robby in every man she has gotten involved with." Then he looked at me. "But remember, Cynthia, it's a child's perception."

Dad said, "I have grieved over the way I treated my family. Back then, when they were children, was a time when parents didn't totally raise their kids. I had so many responsibilities to save that college that my family always came last. But my kids had to be perfect. If I had to use the belt to make them that way, well, so be it. I now realize that Robby just wanted his dad to be home. He wanted a dad to go fishing and hunting with, but I didn't have the time. Whenever I came home from a long business trip, he had gotten into trouble, so I had to punish him. But Cynthia, you were the perfect child. Your mom and I didn't know you needed us. After we punished Robby, we were so drained and hurt that all we could do was go to our own room. Now I wish—and how I have grieved over this—how I wish I would have given more praises to Robby instead of spankings."

"Did you hear that, Cynthia?" Mike asked. "Spankings. Your father didn't *beat* your brother. Were you ever spanked, Cynthia?"

"Never," I said. "Are you kidding? Robby's yelling and pain were enough to let me know that there was no way I would ever be disobedient."

"So why did you think Robby was beaten? Your brother was never beaten like Clint. Your brother was never left at an orphanage like William. He was disciplined. But, do you know why you subconsciously felt he was beaten? Because the only pain you had experienced was from your burns. You see, every time your brother yelled and cried, you subconsciously remembered the burns, the hot water, and the event where the doctors and nurses had to hurt you to help you. That was the only pain you could associate with whenever Robby yelled. Robby was not beaten, but because of your locked-up little girl and her locked-up pain, you thought he must be going through the same pain."

Tears were rolling down my face. "You're right, Mike. I never realized that till now. I didn't know anything about spankings. Poor little Cyndi; why didn't somebody help her?"

"Because you were the perfect child. No one knew you were hurting because you didn't want to bother anyone. So, Cynthia, when did you become damaged freight? But what about the men in your life? Why aren't you married? When did you become damaged freight?"

I recalled a date I had where the guy was opening his heart to me, and really wanting a close relationship. I didn't know how to deal with his openness, and his good looks intimidated me. "How in the world can he go for me?" I thought. He asked me if I wanted children and my reply was, "Yes, someday, but I haven't found anyone I want to make babies with."

Mike looked at me, amazed. "What? You actually told him that? Boy, talk about a heart and ego breaker, you're a classic, Cynthia! Let me tell you why your relationships never work out. Your name is Cyrilla. That's a nickname for a gorilla. I can just see you beating your chest saying, 'Me Cyrilla. I don't need you. Leave me alone. I am self-sufficient and tough enough to stand alone.' Every time a good guy came up to you, I'll bet you looked at him with a screaming look that said, 'It won't work, so just stay away.' If I were single, I wouldn't want to go up to you, Cyrilla. I'd be afraid I would have my teeth kicked in." Once again, Mike took his arm and beat his chest, "'Leave me alone. I'm too overwhelming. I'm damaged freight. It won't work. My name Cyrilla.' Talk about vibes!"

I was in tears, but we were all laughing, because Mike was right. I have been like a gorilla. I never needed men after all. Dad was never there, Matthew left me, William left me, and every other man would probably leave me, so why even try?

Then I remembered other scenes. My girlfriend and I would be sitting in a restaurant or out somewhere, and, invariably, guys would walk up to me and say, "Would you introduce me to your girlfriend?"

I used to tell them in essence to back off. If they wanted to meet her, they talked to her. I always stood by.

Once when this had happened too many times, she and I walked out of the restaurant. I was in tears, and I asked her what was wrong with me. Was I that ugly? She told me no, I just didn't know how to flirt. But I didn't care to flirt. I was disdainful when I thought of batting my eyes.

Mike laughed and said, "You're going to have a special assignment with the group tomorrow, Cynthia."

My parents and I were getting the message. First, I would have to break away from them as parents and from the idea of saving the family. Mike made me introduce myself as adult Cynthia; they were Bob and Joye, my parents, but now my friends. I went on to tell Dad that I wanted him to brag about me if the occasion were appropriate. "You see, Dad, I'm okay whether you think it or not. And from now on, you are not going to comment about my body. If I'm fat, if I'm skinny, or if I'm in between, if I have zits or a clear complexion, you are going to accept me as I am. You are going to love me no matter how I look. And if you are proud of me, I want you to tell people. All my life you never talked about me. Well, I want that to change."

Dad said I was right. "You have to understand that I was in the limelight a lot, and I was responsible for so many people and jobs I never wanted to be found guilty of bragging about my own child. But Cynthia, if I had a piece of clay, I could not have molded a finer daughter than you. I have always been proud of you."

"I know all that, Dad, but I want to see some healthy open admiration of your daughter. God made me. I am not a piece of junk. I am *not* damaged freight."

There, I said it. I realized Mike was trying to get me to say it all this time. The thought was buried. If my parents weren't there when I was burned, in pain, being "raped," if Dad was never around while I was growing up, if my parents were concerned about my scars, and if the messages were always, "You're not good enough," it was no wonder I felt like damaged freight. But I need feel that way no longer.

Dad said, "I know I have failed in many ways. I should have been with my children instead of saving the world. Then I was so wrapped up in Robby's life I had no idea that my 'perfect daughter' was hurting too."

"Oh, Daddy, I never knew, either. I mean, I always felt so misplaced, but I didn't really know I felt all this stuff toward you until I got so sick. Daddy, I love you."

"My sweet Cyndi, I love you more than life."

Our session was over. Mom and Dad left. Everything was going to be okay; or was it? I still had turmoil inside and wondered what was happening to me.

15

Scarred

Mom and Dad were gone, but the next day I was still emotional. I felt big and ugly, and hopeless. I hated myself and told the group about it.

"They are making me eat here and I can't get it out of my body. I want to curl up and die," I sobbed. "I can't stand all these foods in my body. I can't stand myself. Don't you understand? I hate myself."

"The burns, Cynthia. Tell us again about the burns."

I didn't want to go through that again, but I did. The memories came of the push, the water falling on me, my screaming, the emergency room, my waking up to find strange people wrapping my waist down to my legs. There were toothpicks sticking out of my legs, which were really my peeling skin. There was the loneliness.

Then another memory came. I was thirsty and asked the nurse for some grape juice. She said, "If I give you some, you'll just throw up." She sounded mean, but she gave me some anyway. Sure enough, I threw up all over my bed. When the nurse came back, she yelled, "I told you, little girl, you'd throw up, and look at the mess!"

She cleaned it up, angry at me the whole time. The smell was awful but the nurse said I deserved the smell. She said I was a bad girl, a bad girl, a bad girl.

I opened my eyes. My body hurt. I heard other sobs mingling with mine—Tab's. She said, "I know how Cynthia feels. I feel ugly and worthless, too. I remember when I was in the hospital in Germany. I had lost too much weight and they locked me up in a room and wouldn't let anyone come and see me. The nurses told me I was a bad girl. I thought I must be bad. After all, my parents never came to see me."

Mike said, "So that's why you lost two pounds this week, huh, Tab?"

"What? I lost weight?"

"Oh, no," I thought. "She was sixty-seven pounds. That means she's now sixty-five pounds." I started sobbing.

"What's wrong, Cynthia?" Mike asked.

"Tab is going to die. She could die. Tab, please don't die."

Tab was sobbing. "Oh, God, I don't want to die."

Mike yelled out, "You do, too. Look at you. You're shaking your legs to burn up calories, and you do that every time I look at you. Tell me, Tab, how many calories are you burning up?"

Tab cried out, "I didn't realize it until now, but you are right. I do shake my legs all the time. At night I shake and shake, I'm so afraid of getting fat."

"You're dying for Daddy, Tab," Mike retorted. Daddy wanted a boy, not a little girl."

Tab sobbed, "You're right. He told me I was supposed to be a little boy, not a girl. My sister is athletic and Daddy is proud of her. I can't do any masculine athletics. I love ballet."

I asked Tab, "Did your dad ever go to see you in a performance?"

"No, he was always too busy." Tab's father was an army general. She never got mad at him because he said it was disrespectful.

"That's the way my dad was. He was never there when I performed in a play or won an award."

Mike glared at both of us and said, "Oh, Daddy really has you two women. Tab is neuter and Cynthia is afraid of being a woman."

"But I don't want to live for Daddy any more," I said.

Tab said, "I don't know what to do. All I want is for Dad to respect me. He blames me for everything. He says I'm selfish, and my anorexia is my fault. He told me to always keep my mouth shut, and especially not to talk about him here. 'Tab, if you don't have anything to say, keep your mouth shut.'" Tab continued to mimic her dad's unreasonable and cruel yelling at her.

Would our fathers always be such an influence on our lives?

After the session, Sam talked to me. "I want to tell you something. If you believe in God, then you must believe in Satan. I see it like this. You have two bidders in your life. God bids for your life. You are committed to him totally. In return, he'll give you strength, a life forever. But Satan is also bidding for you. He has given you bulimia, an easy way to keep a thin body to serve him. You, Cynthia, must tell the auctioneer which one you want to buy your life."

Two bidders. Oh, God, please don't let Satan buy my soul.

At 11 P.M. I walked into the day room after a perfectly enjoyable evening out with Carrie and Steven. There was a big bag of cookies on the table. My monster said. "But, Cynthia, you are not supposed to feel good. Go ahead and destroy yourself." The old bulimic, secretive, manipulative Cynthia emerged. I made sure no one was watching. I got twelve of those big cookies and stuffed them into my pocket, then down my throat. Suddenly I panicked. "What have I done? I've got to get rid of this junk in my stomach." I sat down, and my cheerful self became hateful and gloomy.

Steven noticed. "Cynthia, what's wrong?"

"Nothing, Steven. Leave me alone."

Steven came and put his arms around me. "What is wrong?"

"Oh, Steven," the tears came. "I just ate some cookies."

"So what? What's a couple of cookies going to do?"

"But it wasn't a couple. I lost control and ate twelve. Or maybe it was fifteen, and now I can't get rid of them."

"Don't feel guilty," he said. "I agree fifteen is too many, but don't feel guilty."

I left and went to my room to be alone. I was no good. Why couldn't I believe I was worthwhile?

But, when I awakened the next morning, I decided it was a new day and time to start over.

I told the group about the cookies of the night before. I said there was a part of me that one moment felt deserving of a good feeling, and the next moment I was self-destructive.

Mike said, "That's a good setup, Cynthia."

I wasn't sure what he meant, but I related how every time a friend asked me out, say on a Saturday night or to go on a trip, I would say yes. But then, the night before, I would binge and purge, or take laxatives on an empty stomach after starving myself for three days, and I'd be sick. I would always cancel the plans. Was that a setup?

"Yep. That's a classic."

Carrie, too, had binged the evening before. But her reason was to gain the weight she feared she'd lost, so she would be allowed a pass to go home that day. Carrie had been in the hospital two months, and her weight had dropped from 140 pounds to 115. Now she was saying she would be happy if she could lose another 10 pounds. Her obsession with her body and with losing weight obscured her emotions of anger and sadness; being assertive was scary, so she concentrated on being skinny.

I again relived my obsession of not being good enough, so why bother to be involved with people, and why not just go ahead and destroy myself with food and laxatives and vomiting and starvation. I wasn't supposed to have a good time, and didn't deserve love from Carrie and Steven.

Afterward, Sam again wanted to talk with me. "I want you to know I love you, no matter what. You are worthwhile. If you stick that in your heart when Satan or the monster wants to destroy you, I think it will help you. Before you take those cookies, think about my concern for you, because what you really need is love and someone to tell you, 'You are special.'"

"Oh, Sam," I said. "Thank you. I so badly want to believe you."

I had a pass to go out with Brenda following her outpatient session. As we walked through the lobby, Clint was sitting in the waiting room with Steven. He didn't speak as we passed. When I looked at him he wasn't the Clint I thought I knew. He was suddenly very ugly to me. Why was I ever attracted to this man? Mike had indicated the answer: Clint had potential. Did I ever feel stupid for having been attracted to Clint. But I thanked God that it had happened, for by means of Clint I finally learned that my pattern with men was that I was trying to save my brother through them. Well, never again.

Brenda seemed to be doing well. However, she told me that she binged and threw up once that week. "Cynthia, it was so strange. I had to do it. It was as though I was so perfect being a cured bulimic that I had to do it and see how it felt. Well, after I did it, I asked myself, 'Why in the world did I do this for fourteen years?'"

The conversation scared me. "Do you think it will ever happen again?"

"No, because I realized it just wasn't worth it."

Brenda's children were with us. I adored them. Her little girl was full of life. She talked to me and asked me questions. It made me feel special when she wrapped her little arms around me.

Back at the hospital, Carrie, Steven, and I had planned to go shopping together, but only Steven was waiting for me. He said Carrie had changed her mind and went home instead. I asked who took Carrie home, and he said Clint.

"Clint! Oh, Steven, no!" I hadn't told him what I'd learned about Clint. Steven hadn't noticed that Carrie and Clint spent a lot of time together right before Clint left the ward. Then Steven started thinking about the conversation he and Clint had before I came to pick him up.

"He was weird, Cynthia. Stupid me, I just didn't connect anything. He said he was there to see Brenda."

"Brenda? No way. Clint and Brenda were in their outpatient group together this morning. Brenda and I walked right past you guys. Something strange is going on. I'm scared. Did Carrie tell you she was going with Clint? And why did she suddenly decide not to go with us?"

Steven got worried. So did I. "You know, he really bad mouthed his wife. Then he said, 'I'm going to look for something strange tonight.'"

"That's sick."

"It really is. Guys talk, but I've never heard a guy talk that way."

"Steven, we've got to do something. Let's call the hospital." We called and asked with whom Carrie had checked out. We decided that if she said Clint, then she was responsible; but if she didn't put his name on the checkout sheet, then we'd be really worried. The aide told us over the phone that Carrie had indeed written Clint's name. "Okay, she is responsible for herself." We decided not to worry until we saw her. We didn't have her home phone number, so there wasn't much we could do anyway.

Steven and I went to a movie. It was my first one in over two months, and being in the theater bothered me. Flashbacks of movies I had gone to over the years came to me, and of my sitting alone eating candy bars, hot dogs and popcorn, and popping pills between bites of food.

Please, God, don't let that happen ever again.

When we got back to the hospital it was obvious Carrie was spending the night with her parents. We hoped that Clint wouldn't do anything rash.

In the morning Steven and I went to church together. It was a good service. The minister talked about childhood and parents and how important it is to love children and tell them about God. It was the first service Steven had been to in a long time, and his face perspired the whole time.

We went to brunch and I ate too much. I went past the full signal and was then guilt ridden. I took a nap to escape. My sleep was awful. I got the shakes and had visions of all that food and what it was doing to me: making me fat.

Tab awakened me to tell me dinner was ready, which irritated me. But it wasn't Tab I was angry with; I was angry at myself for eating so much at brunch. The food was now stuck between my stomach and throat. I wanted to throw up. Why did I feel so guilty about eating? I hated my body.

Carrie was late for the Sunday evening group session. I was so angry I couldn't speak to her. Afterward, Steven and I told her the story about Clint and me, and how worried we were about her. She was stunned. It turned out that Clint had given her the same lines he had given me: poor Clint; my wife is so mean; I don't get anything from my wife; Oh, Carrie, you are so special; I've never met a girl like you. Carrie was frightened when Steven told her about Clint's talk of looking for something strange. She and Clint had spent the day together and ended up eating dinner with her parents.

"Did he do anything to you, Carrie?" I asked.

"He kissed me."

"Carrie, Clint is a married man! He has a wife to go home to, and he knows you are vulnerable and still sick. He wanted to use you. Thank God, he didn't try anything else."

Carrie started crying. She said she liked Clint and wanted to be with him, but was ashamed he had used her. She promised to never see him again. She said she had never had friends like Steven and me. Her other friends abused her rather than becoming concerned about her. Guys she dated beat up on her, used her, treated her like a dog.

Steven and I proclaimed our love for Carrie and she expressed her love for us. The three of us hugged each other tightly. We were going to make it!

I went to bed early, but felt lonely and depressed, even though I knew I was loved. What was wrong with me?

Ike stunned me when he apologized for his anger toward me. He said he hated it when I would talk in the group, because it seemed I was doing it all for attention.

I was hurt, but I had to respond. "Maybe you're just jealous, Ike, because I'm really expressing how I feel. I never hear you talk about your feelings or your experiences. Well, I do talk. I'm not in here to sit on my can!"

"Yes, I'm jealous of you, Cynthia. You're not afraid of getting it all out. I'm insecure around you. You remind me of my aunt."

"What did your aunt do to you?" I asked.

"She always made me feel like a little kid."

"Well, I'm not your aunt, Ike. You know, last night I was so depressed. You saw that, as I walked down the hall, I needed to talk to you. You knew I was down, but no, you didn't care."

Mike asked, "Why didn't you think Ike wanted to talk to you?"

"Because I never think a guy like Ike would approach me. It's like you say, Mike, I silently scream, 'It won't work.'"

"What is there about Ike that you don't think you deserve?" Mike asked.

"He's handsome, kind, genuine. When he finds his niche, I know he'll make it in this world."

"Ike, did you know Cynthia felt that way?" Mike asked.

"I had no idea. I always felt inferior to Cynthia."

"Why are you damaged freight, Cynthia?" Mike asked again.

"I hate my body. I am so ugly, so fat. I'm scarred." I was rocking and pounding my knees.

"When did you become damaged freight, Cynthia?"

Again tears came, and memories of being pushed, the hot water, the skin peeling, the doctors and nurses hurting my thighs, no one there, and now I'm scarred for life. I must have cried for fifteen minutes.

Mike yelled at me, "Cynthia, say, *The accident was not my fault. I am not damaged freight.* Say it now, Cynthia."

I yelled, "The accident was not my fault. I am not damaged freight." I sobbed, got down on my knees, curled up, and rocked myself.

"Say it again. Tell everyone in this room."

I said it to the new patients, insincerely, "The accident was not my fault. I am not damaged freight." But when I looked at Sam, Carrie, Tab, Ike and Steven, it was hard to say it. While gasping for new breath, I sobbed, "The burns were not my fault. I am not damaged freight."

Ike got out of his chair, held me in his strong arms, and whispered to me, "Cynthia, the accident was not your fault. You are a beautiful woman." I held Ike tightly.

Two hours later the impact of it hit me: I also became damaged freight *after* I was burned, when I became scarred. That's why I'd been abusing my body. If my parents weren't there when I was in such horrid pain, and if they weren't there to protect me from the "abuse" of the doctors and nurses, I must be damaged freight. Destroying my body all those years had protected me from getting involved with a good man, because subconsciously I felt like damaged freight. That was a major cause of my becoming bulimic, why I broke down every time Mike told me to relive the burns. But now I knew, I was *not* damaged freight. I wasn't!

God, thank you for opening my eyes. Please help me to accept what I can't change, and help me change what you want me to change.

16

Peaks and Valleys

I kept praying that God would want me to have a new career when I was well. I did very much want to write a book. My parents were trying to sell my house in Little Rock. I didn't want to go back there, and if it sold I would know God did not want me to go back there. But they had been there for two weeks without success. No one had shown an interest in the house.

God, I want to serve you. I want to tell people about this horrid disease. If my house sells, it will take a lot of pressure off me. It will help pay my hospital bills and relieve my parents. Please, God, could you find someone to buy it?

Mom called the morning after my stormy group session to tell me they'd sold the house. They received only two phone calls on it all week, but that morning someone drove by, saw the for sale sign, and bought it with cash.

God, thank you. I know you really want me to tell people about you.

Please help me to continue believing. Help me to help myself become healed.

Steven told Mike about what happened between Clint and Carrie and me, even though we'd decided to keep it among the three of us. So I wasn't expecting it when Mike stormed into my room and said, "How does it feel to fall for a psychopathic liar?"

I was stunned. "It doesn't feel good, Mike. I had no idea Clint lied so well. I haven't been completely honest with you. He wrote me letters while he was here." Mike looked at them. I told him I, too, had written Clint letters, but not like his, and that now I felt like a total idiot.

Mike said, "I just talked to Carrie about this. Do you know how many women patients on this ward have gotten letters just like this from Clint?"

"No."

"About six, and that doesn't include you and Carrie. Cynthia, run away from men that have been beaten. Got it?"

"Yes, I've got it, Mike. I've got it."

A woman, not in the Minirth-Meier group but whom I saw in the day room, and I talked about our bulimia. She told about not eating all day, but on the way home from work buying six sandwiches and a big jar of pickles. Once while driving she almost choked to death on a pickle. For a while she had kept her secret from her husband of six months, but finally he discovered it and told her she had to get help. They wanted children, but her periods had stopped. She was a fat teenager. Then she watched a movie, "The Best Little Girl in the World," about an anorexic who threw up. That was how this woman started, and then she couldn't stop.

I prayed, "God, lead me to make this public. I will talk about how deadly this disease is, so women won't be tempted to start it."

Lindy, the woman who was bulimic and diabetic, was finally out of the intensive care unit. She maintained she was ready to go home, because she didn't feel like binging. I told her, "Of course, you don't. You're locked up and can't binge. But if you don't deal with yourself and your basic problems and go home now, you will start all over again." I tried to tell both women that food was not the issue; rather, it was how we deal with life.

"You see, if you and I are obsessed with our bodies and being thin all the time, if we are busy fasting, binging, and throwing up, then we don't have to deal with what is really wrong. Believe me, you're bulimic for a lot of reasons." I didn't think they knew what I was talking about.

My minister from church called and told me not to worry about my hospital bill. The church was giving me enough money to stay another three weeks. So, with my house money and the church's aid, I would be able to stay as long as necessary. I thanked God for compassionate Christians.

Before I went to bed I was angry with an aide because he wasn't listening to me. I told him about my finally understanding my trying to be savior of my family, and of looking for my brother in the men I went out with. But he was looking at TV instead of at me. When he did respond, he put me down by saying, "But what about tonight, Cynthia? That was all figured out last week. What about now?"

I was angry, because everything was just beginning to make sense, but I didn't have all the answers yet. I went right to the refrigerator and got out some food. But I stopped and asked myself, "Okay, Cynthia, what really is going on?" I wasn't hungry; I was angry. So I went to the aide and we talked it out. I didn't eat the rest of the night, and it was the first time in twelve years I had that kind of control. Congratulations, Cynthia! I was patting myself on the back.

Elizabeth and I went out together for an evening. It was her first time out with someone besides her parents. We got all dressed up, and she was in a mood for fun. We went to a restaurant and talked about boys and her parents. She embarrassed me by sticking her knife into a jar of honey and licking the knife. I told her if she wanted to go out with me, she'd better use proper manners.

When we returned, I got a phone call from my girlfriend, Jessica.

She said, "Why aren't you here, Cynthia? I thought you would just get some rest and come home after two weeks. It's been a month. I miss you Cynthia. You're my best friend."

The monster was enraged. "So, I'm your best friend, huh? You don't know what a friend is. I was dying right before your very eyes and you did *nothing!* " I screamed.

Then she became angry. "Now, wait a minute. I tried to do something, but you wouldn't talk to me. You wouldn't let me do anything. What was I supposed to do? Put you on the floor with my foot on your neck and hold you there for twenty-four hours a day?"

"Yes, if that's what it took. You don't understand what I've lived with and what I'm going through. Good-bye." The tears were coming and I was shaking. Forget it.

When I crawled into bed, Elizabeth was joking around with me and I was even laughing. Then suddenly the abundant alone feeling engulfed me and my mind told me to kill myself. If I'd had a gun, right then I would have blown my brain all over the wall. "Oh, God, please, no, no," I yelled. "I don't want that!"

Elizabeth said, "Please, Cynthia, don't feel that way. If you'd die, I'd die. Go talk to someone."

I got up to talk to a nurse. Everyone was busy getting ready to leave but the next shift hadn't arrived yet. "Please, please, somebody help me."

Everyone said, "Wait another thirty minutes, Cynthia. We're too busy."

"Too busy? Look, I want to blow my brains out. Somebody had better have time for me. Please, please," I screamed. "I don't want to die."

Everyone looked shaken. One of my favorite nurses took me into a room. "Oh, why do I have these horrible thoughts of wanting to end my life? Please help me. I don't want to die."

She held me. "Cynthia, what are you thinking? Describe it."

"It's that I'm figuring out my life, but it hurts so badly to realize that for twenty-eight years I've been miserable. I feel so crushed, so angry at being sick while no one knew."

"Cynthia, the little girl in you is grieving. She has been dead for so long, so allow her to grieve."

"Oh, Sandy," I cried, as she held me, "I want to live, not die." She gave me a sleeping pill, and I slept fitfully.

While I was eating breakfast Mike came and beckoned me into a private room.

"Mike, why does a part of me want to kill myself? I am scared. For twenty-eight years I've been so empty, and now that I'm becoming healed I still feel death penetrating my soul."

"That is because you have convinced yourself you will never be happy, that you don't deserve to be happy."

I sobbed, "I have been sick for so long, and no one noticed."

"You have a great facade, Cynthia."

"But Mike, I told my close friends I felt I was dying, and now they say, 'Why is it taking you so long to get well?'"

"Say it, Cynthia. Say you're angry at them for not noticing you."

"Yes, I'm angry." I yelled. Mike got a foam rubber beating bat and pointed to the chair. "I don't want to, Mike."

"Get up," he said, "and beat all those people you're angry at, who never helped you. You can never forgive them until you become aware of the vengeance you are already feeling toward them."

I hit and hit the chair. I sobbed and screamed, "Why didn't you listen to me? Why didn't you see that I was dying?" I hit Mom, Dad, Robby, my girlfriend. My back and sides were aching. I must have hit the chair for thirty minutes. I was sweating and my heart was pounding.

I sat down, exhausted, and sobbed, and heaved, and shook for a long time.

Finally, Mike asked, "What's going on Cynthia?"

"I was just thinking about a few months ago. I was seriously considering killing myself. I went out on a story and saw a man whose daughter had shot herself in the head. I hurt for that man. I thought about my dad and how deeply I'd hurt him if I killed myself. Seeing that man stopped me that day from taking my life."

I sobbed some more.

"Now what's going on, Cynthia?"

"My brother called me the first week I was here. He told me that there have been many times he has put the gun to his head ready to pull the trigger, but having his two babies kept him from going through with it."

"It sounds like you and Robby have a death pact. Tell me, is it a fantasy that your parents find you with your brains blown out?"

"No, Mike, I don't want to hurt them."

"Oh, come on, you do too. Wouldn't it be wonderful to be dead and have your dad, who never was there, find you, and the message to him when he saw you dead would be, 'See, I was really sick, and where were you?' Fantasy, Cynthia, pure fantasy. Punishment, revenge on those people who didn't know you were sick. What a great facade you had."

"On the phone last night, my friend told me, 'Cynthia, you came to work, you smiled, you talked, you produced great stories, you looked good on camera. How was I supposed to know you were dying?'" I realized it wasn't Jessica's fault for not helping me. I never told her how desperately I needed help.

"What a great facade." Mike got up to leave the room, "I expect you to talk about this with the group." He walked out. My body ached.

When I walked out the door, the other patients looked frightened. They had heard me screaming. Ole Cynthia had scared everyone. I did not want to talk to the group about my suicidal thoughts.

Mike's lecture was on feelings. He explained that we all came to that ward because suddenly our conscious selves had quit. We couldn't bear our problems any longer, so our subconscious selves took over.

To be suicidal means part of you is a killer and part of you wants to be killed. Suicidal thoughts come because you have suppressed too much into your subconscious, which gets overloaded. It, in turn, says, "Get this junk out of here or you will die."

Mike looked straight at me and said, "Tell us what happened to you last night."

I said, "I felt like dying last night. Mike made me realize I was angry at those who are close to me and love me, but who didn't see I was sick. He made me use the beating stick and scream at those I was angry with, and then forgive them."

"Suicidal thoughts are anger turned inward. Today, the hitting was anger turned outward, and no one was hurt. You're not dead right now, are you?" Mike looked at me with his strange look that made me freeze and think, "What is going on?"

That evening I ate six cookies and a bagel. I didn't know what I was doing.

God, help me!

17

The Setup

Eleven forty-five A.M., Day 53—my body was working, my bowels were working. It felt so good for my bowels to be normal, I thanked the Lord.

Dr. Gutierrez told me he was impressed by my perception of various people in group therapy. It was true, I was beginning to realize that when people treated me badly, it was not always my fault. Sometimes they were having problems. I planned to do more reaching out to other people.

I told Dr. Gutierrez about my desire to die, to kill myself. He said maybe it was because I would soon have to leave the hospital.

After years of searching for answers about myself, I was finally getting them from people who cared about me. "After all, you will be leaving Mike, and it's taken you over ten years to find someone who could save your life."

"Oh, come on, Dr. Gutierrez, leaving Mike is no big deal." It irritated me he said that. What did dying have to do with my therapist?

I went to talk to an aide and told her I wanted help, because I was confused. She just looked at me coldly and said, "Give up your control, Cynthia. You are one tough lady, and you always want to be in control." What did that mean, give up control? I was more confused.

The rest of the staff members, too, were acting strangely. It seemed they were bent on criticizing me. One of the aides told me he thought I was doing a con job on my parents and my church by asking for money to help pay for my hospital bills. "What are you talking about? My money is none of your business."

"Oh, but it is if you are ripping people off."

"Look, I wish I didn't have to ask for help, but I did have to. Why are you accusing me?"

"I don't think you know why you're in this hospital."

I was sick to my stomach. Maybe he was right. I was no good. I shouldn't have asked anyone for help, but found a way by myself. But where could I have gotten the money? Then he said that maybe my having no money would be an excuse to not eat. He was so cruel, I wanted to run away and die. I didn't understand.

Rachel, my favorite aide, had been away for a two-week vacation, and I was glad to see her back. But she seemed distant. I asked her about it, and she said the staff told her I hadn't been cooperating or working on my problems while she was gone. She said she was disappointed in me. I was crushed. "What are you talking about? I've been working hard." I told her all I had discovered about myself, but I could see she didn't believe me. I was furious.

I stormed into my session with Mike. He had me sit and talk about my anger, but he didn't say much. I told Mike about the absurdity of Dr. Gutierrez's remark about my feeling suicidal because I was going to leave him. His eyes were penetrating, and he remarked coolly, "Well, think about it, I am the only therapist who has pushed your emotional buttons. You will leave here and won't have me to push your buttons. How does that grab you?"

"I don't want to die, Mike. I really don't," I cried.

Next I found out somebody wrote on my chart that I'd raided the dinner trays one night. That wasn't true! I was trading my meal for the salad of someone who was out on a pass. I was not raiding trays. The staff members wrote that I was not working, that I was not going to make it, that I wasn't talking about myself, that I was playing therapist with everyone else. That wasn't true either. I worked all day long, I talked, I listened, I cried, I ached, and lived my sorrow. Marta, the occupational therapist, and the nurses all criticized me. But probably they were right. I was no good.

Throughout the night I worried. I had been there close to eight weeks and they said I wasn't working, that I talked only to the patients. I had to figure it out or I couldn't go on living.

Before breakfast the next morning I made appointments with three nurses and three aides. They all criticized me. "Why are you going out to eat tonight? Why are you so close to your fourteen-year old roommate? Why are you, Steven, and Carrie such a clique? Why do you play therapist? Do you know that everyone would give their eyeteeth to be your roommate after Elizabeth leaves? Why do you say you may write a book? Are you playing reporter here in the psych ward?" Even though no one actually said it, I *thought* they meant, "You are no good, Cynthia."

I went to Dr. Gutierrez with tears in my eyes. "I don't want to play therapist, but I don't know what is good or bad, right or wrong." Kind, gentle Dr. Gutierrez said, "This is good, Cynthia. Your feelings may be surfacing." My only feelings were pain and confusion.

When Mike questioned me, I said, "I'm so confused about myself. A therapist told me last year I would have to be hospitalized to overcome this, but I totally rejected that. I'll figure it all out myself, thank you. Now I know I was not listening." I started sobbing. "Oh, I have blown my whole life. I started going with my ex-husband the second week of my freshman year in college, and I was with him, only him, in school for three lousy years. I missed so many opportunities because I had to have only one person in my life. I missed out on college life. Those years were wasted; three of the best years of my life were lost. And during the last ten years I cannot tell you when I was happy. My whole life I have been so miserable; I have always been alone."

Mike was in one of his sarcastic moods, but I didn't care. He asked me, "How did you feel when the staff was coming down on you?"

"Well, some of it I appreciated," I answered meekly.

Mike snickered. "You appreciated it? Three nights ago you wanted to blow your brains out. You don't talk about it to the group. An aide that has been on vacation for two weeks says ten people say you haven't been working, and you appreciate it?" I couldn't talk, I was so afraid.

After the group had left the room and I was alone, one of the aides came over and hugged me and said, "It's okay to be afraid, Cynthia." I didn't understand anything. I went to occupational therapy to draw. Mike came in and stared at me. The occupational therapist stood by him. All of a sudden they started blasting me with sarcasm. Oh, how it hurt. Mike looked at Marta, "Cynthia, here, gets beaten all over by the staff and she takes it. Can you believe that?"

Marta said, "On pass she eats out. She doesn't get her assignments done here. I don't think she's working."

Mike added, "Yet, she wants to blow her brains out. I think we should restrict her from going out ever."

"Then do it!" I yelled. "Everyone says I'm not working, but I am. I don't want to die. Why are you doing this? I want to work, and if I'm not, please help me change."

Mike said, "I never said you weren't working! I'm your therapist." He looked at Marta and said, "I think Cynthia is dealing with secondary issues, not primary issues."

"Oh, please," I cried. "What is the primary issue? I'm self-destructive but I don't want to be. I'm here because I want to be rid of the horrible monster that is trying to kill me. I can't leave here and be bulimic. I cannot live in that agony when I get out." The tears were streaming and I used my sleeve to wipe my nose. I rocked with my arms wrapped around me.

Mike asked, "What are you rocking for, Cynthia?" I stopped. He seemed to be criticizing me. "What are you rocking for?" he repeated sarcastically.

"I don't know, Mike," I screamed at him. "I guess because it's comforting."

"Comforting, huh? Is that what you need? Comfort? How do you get comfort, Cynthia?"

Marta said, "Maybe that's her problem. She doesn't know how to get comfort."

"I don't know. I don't know." Why was Mike harassing me? I put my head in my hands to escape the pain. I wanted to get out of his world and die.

Someone touched me at that point. Mike put his arms around me; then Marta came and embraced me. They both engulfed me with their warm bodies. "How does this feel, Cynthia?" Was that compassion I heard in Mike's voice? The touch and the warmth were comforting. "Comfort. Is this comfort?" Mike asked as we three rocked together.

"Yes."

"Cynthia, go to everyone right now and say, 'I need comfort.'"

I did. "Randy, I need comfort," I said.

Randy took me in his strong arms and my head rested on his shoulder. It felt good to embrace. "I care about you, Cynthia. I'll give you comfort."

"Carrie, I need comfort."

There were tears, sobs, more warm embraces, wonderful human warmth from Sam, Tab, Rachel, and the others.

I was fulfilled but still confused. I went to my room, and Carrie followed. "Oh, Carrie, I'm so confused. I don't understand what that was all about. Mike and Marta were so mean to me. What is happening?

Before she could respond there was a knock on my door. It was Steven. He was crying! Steven had not cried since he was twelve years old. He took Carrie's and my hands, looked at us and said, "How I love you two. You're the first women that I have ever loved, the first ladies that I have truly, deeply cared about."

We three embraced and cried with tears of joy, confusion, and some fear. But it was at this moment I knew that we were going to live.

A few days before, someone in our group had said that Carrie, Steven, and I thought we were too good for the others on the ward. It was true that we had opened our hearts to each other and reached out. We had learned to be willing to be vulnerable, to openly give and receive each other's love. Each of the "top three"—Carrie, Steven and I—would die for the other two friends.

That night, Ike, Steven, and I went to a Texas Rangers baseball game. Ike said he felt good and wanted me to feel that way. I honestly tried to have a good time, but I was depressed and drained. I didn't understand why everyone had been so critical of me, particularly Mike and Marta. Yet, I agreed with their criticisms.

On the way home, Steven and I were in the back seat of Ike's car. I cried and cried, and Steven put his arms around me. "I thought I had been working in the hospital, but the staff says I haven't. But I've been working."

"Look," Steven said, "I know you've been working, Carrie knows you have. Mike said you've been working, and he's the guy who's saving your life."

Before I went to bed, Ryun hugged me and said, "I love you."

"Oh, Ryun, I love you, too. I just don't know how to love myself."

My sleep was a struggle. There was no peace.

I woke up crying. In the day room, I was still crying when Dr. Gutierrez came to me. I told him about the previous day. "This is good. Your feelings are surfacing," he said.

When he left, one of the nurses said, "Come on, Cynthia. Let's go to your room and talk." We sat on my bed. "What's going on?" she asked.

"Mike has been harassing me all week. I'm realizing that Cynthia Rowland has needs, but it is hard to talk about them."

"What does everyone in this world need? What does every living soul want?" she asked.

"Love."

"That's right."

A spark lit up inside me. I rushed to the room where group therapy was beginning. I was angry. I looked at Rachel, the aide who had been on vacation for two weeks. I thought of the accusations she had made, saying I was not working. I looked straight at her and said, "You had no right, Rachel, to accuse me. You should have asked me and seen for yourself how I was doing, before reporting to me what the staff thought. I *have* been working. I don't want to die, I want to live."

"But that's what the staff told me," Rachel answered. "They said you were not working."

"Well, then the staff wasn't working. When I wanted to blow my head off last week, I went to them crying for help and they told me they were too busy to talk to me, they had charts to do. So I demanded it. I wanted to kill myself and they were fooling with charts. Furthermore, your fellow aide that accused me of ripping off the church because it is helping with my bill is full of hogwash. I need help. If I had left that week my insurance ran out, I would not be making it. I cared enough about me and my health to ask for help, and I'm proud of myself for having the courage to say I'm sick and need help desperately. We're talking about Christian people who love me, and they want me to be healed."

"You'r right," she said. "I see that now. Please forgive me for not checking everything out with you before I accused you."

My fellow patients were grinning and applauding me. Ike said, "Cynthia, don't feel ashamed that you asked for help. I too, had to get some financial help from my church. That's what my church is all about—giving to those in need."

"You're right, Ike, and I've been too proud to ask for help. I have always been taught to trust in God and everything will be all right. But God gave us each other, people to reach out to, and he gave us mouths to say, 'I need.'" Tears came. "I want everyone in here to know I need you desperately. I need your love, your comfort, your friendship, your wisdom, and right now I need some hugs." I went around the room and hugged everyone.

Now I understood what Mike had been saying. How could anyone know my needs if I didn't tell them? It was acceptable to tell people, and if the first person rejected me, I could go to the next and the next until I got what I needed. All my life I'd had needs, but I was never taught to acknowledge them. I never wanted to bother anyone. Now I understood that when I became damaged freight at four years old, it was because of my perception that Mom and Dad didn't love me. They were not there when I was burned and hurting. So I was never going to bother anyone by making myself not need anyone. I was dying inside all those years because I was determined to do everything by myself. But no longer. From now on I would acknowledge my dependence on other people.

This was why Mike had treated me the way he did, and it was all a setup by the staff. Just because they said I wasn't working didn't mean it was true. In one of his lectures Mike had said that when you are criticized, you have four choices: 1) to believe what people say, and think you are a bad person; 2) to accept the criticism as truth, and work on the problem; 3) to reject what people say, and tell them why their criticism is not correct; 4) to put the criticism on a shelf and say, "Let me think about that, and I'll get back to you."

I remembered the nurse who accused me of always being friends with anorexics and teenagers, especially Elizabeth. I went to her and said, "I've been thinking about what you said about Elizabeth, and I want you to know, I have not really been friendly only with the kids; I'm enjoying getting to know everyone, because I have been starved for friends."

I went to the aide who accused me of ripping off the church, and told him I was proud of myself for asking for help, and that I was loved enough to receive it. I went to the nurse who accused me of being a reporter on the psychiatric ward. I told her reporting was my career, being perceptive was a gift from God, and I was proud of myself for understanding and caring about people. I went to the aide who accused me of playing therapist, looked him in the eye, and said, "I care about everyone on this floor, and I care enough to ask them thought-provoking questions. Maybe you ought to ask yourself if you're jealous."

Well done. I was assertive. While everyone may not have agreed with my comments, at least I had said my piece. I began to think my heart was connecting with my mind. I was reaching out, touching, talking, feeling, becoming comfortable with myself. I just might make it after all.

Thank you, God, for helping me to need, to love, to keep feeling.

18

My Friends

My aunt, uncle, and cousin came to visit. I was self-conscious, for my skin was an unnatural color and I still looked sick. We went to a shopping mall; I became weak and silently asked God to heal my body.

They revealed something I'd not known for over ten years. The night before my wedding, my cousin, then fourteen years old, heard Matthew tell a friend that he had gotten a girl pregnant and just couldn't marry me.

I was incredulous. Why hadn't my cousin told me? He was too afraid and did not know what to do at the time. If only he had said something, maybe I wouldn't have suffered so much.

Matthew married the girl right after our divorce, and they had the baby a few months later, but I always thought it was my fault the marriage ended. Now it was obvious Matthew had married me because I was a good little Christian girl. His parents wanted him out of their hair and thought I might be his savior, his therapist. But never again would I try to be anyone's therapist or social worker.

I told the group what I'd just learned about Matthew. Dr. Gutierrez asked me if I ever felt suicidal over Matthew. He had been married six months and had the baby before my friends told me. "Yes, I wanted to get a gun then," I said.

Carrie said she felt the same way when her fiance broke up with her. She had told herself that she would love him forever and there would never be anyone else in her life.

Dr. Gutierrez asked "Whom would you hurt if you both blew your brains out?"

"Them," I said.

"But if they loved you, they would not have left you. Do you really think they would have cared if you killed yourselves? Whom would you really end up punishing?"

I looked at Dr. Gutierrez and said, "Only me." He was saying that suicidal thoughts are anger turned inward.

For our outing we went to the park. It was a beautiful sunny day. Ike, Steven, Ryun, Liz, Marta, and I played frisbee.

Liz was a new friend, depressed and going through a divorce. She was worried that her daughter was bulimic. At the college she attended it was a fad to binge and purge. A fad! If they only knew they could become addicted and possibly die.

God, when I am healed help me to reach those women and tell them about the agony of bulimia.

While Marta was talking, Steven was expressionless. "Steven, I am going to figure out a way to give you feeling," I thought. I had a glass of lemonade, and I got a look of glee in my eye. However, Steven also had a glass of lemonade, and all of a sudden he had that look of glee. He came over and I said, "Don't, Steven." Instantly, my lemonade was all over him.

He looked shocked. Suddenly, I felt cold, wet lemonade all over my head, neck and back. Steven was laughing; I was laughing.

Steven said, "Hey, for the first time I don't feel guilty. That was an absolute joy to dump lemonade all over you. It feels good to laugh.

After the laughter I saw a child playing. A memory came to me that I shared with everyone. When I was about seven, my family went to a picnic with a lot of people. While playing, I fell on rocks and skinned my knees and legs. I was bleeding. I cried and cried but no one came. On the way home I was lying on the back seat still crying. I was hurting, but Dad yelled at me and told me to stop crying and be quiet.

Marta said, "Oohh, let's give Cynthia a hug for the time no one came to comfort her when she skinned her knees." Everyone came and hugged me and said, "Ooh, poor Cynthia." We laughed together and the painful memory faded away. The little girl was smiling.

On the way home we stopped for ice cream. It was an hour before dinner, but I wasn't hungry. I had no desire to eat ice cream. Did that ever feel good! The thought of all the gallons of ice cream I had consumed over the years made me sick to my stomach.

When we returned, Mike wanted to see me. He had the funny look in his eye that told me I was going to get it.

I told him about having fun at the park.

He changed the subject. "Have you talked to your mom lately?"

"No, but she writes me every day."

Mike looked straight at me and said, "Isn't it strange to you that during the session with your parents she hardly said a word?"

"I hadn't really thought about it. That's just the way she is," I replied.

"No, I don't think so," Mike said. "Your mom is jealous of you. I think you'd better consider a session with just you and her."

I was surprised. My mom jealous? I didn't believe it. I'd always been jealous of her, she was so small and beautiful. Dad would say things like, "If you would eat like your mother, you would look like your mother." I thought if I could look like Mom, maybe Dad would pay more attention to me.

Now here we were back to bodies. I had been trying to shed that obsession. And it was always, "Your parents, your parents."

Something was wrong with Steven. He looked horrible when I walked into the day room. "Steven, what's wrong?"

He handed me some papers; they would release his baby for adoption. His girlfriend did not want the baby, and she didn't want Steven to keep it, either. Steven looked at me and yelled, "No, no, no, I am not going to give up this baby." He ran out of the room.

When I couldn't find him I went to get Carrie, and we looked all over for him. We finally found him sitting down by the little creek on the hospital grounds, pondering, and looking bewildered. When he saw us coming he ran to us. The "top three" embraced.

"We'll work this out, Steven. Please don't run from us. We love you and want what is best for you." We sat down.

"I don't want to give up this baby. I've given up on one already, and I can't do it again. I feel such guilt about the first baby." Steven started crying. "I was only sixteen and a real druggie. Oh, I was sick. My girlfriend and I decided to abort the baby by injecting the strongest heroin I could find. As I stuck the needle into her arm I became jealous. I thought no way would she and the baby get that heroin. They would experience the high of the drug and I wouldn't.

"So I took the needle out of her arm and stuck it in my arm. Can you believe it? I was going to kill my baby and maybe my girlfriend, but I wanted the drug to get high myself." Steven was sobbing. "Don't you understand? I gave that baby up for adoption after I nearly killed it. I cannot give up this child. I'm free of drugs. I'm going to get well. I want to love that baby."

Steven already had a twelve-year-old daughter to raise. I said, "You have to work to live. How can you be the father you want to be, work, take care of the household, and raise a baby? And what about your daughter? She will be the one that will have to raise the baby. She is only twelve years old. Is that fair?"

"I don't know what's fair any more. I think my mom could raise the baby for me while I work. I just don't know, I feel so lost. I want that baby."

Mike could tell something was wrong when we got to our group. Steven sat in the hot seat and told Mike about the adoption papers.

"OK, Steven," Mike said, "put the baby in the chair and let's talk about it."

Steven looked at the chair, "It's a little boy, a baby boy."

"Yes, your baby boy is right here in the chair wrapped up in a blue blanket. Talk to it." Steven looked at the imagined baby boy and said softly, "Oh, I want you so badly. All my life I've been waiting for you, a boy. I'm going to be the best father I possibly can. I'll be there when you need me. I'm going to be your friend. Together we'll talk and grow. You're going to play baseball, and you'll be good, I know. I'll be there to coach you."

Mike asked me, "Cynthia, what do you think about this conversation between Steven and his baby boy?"

"I don't feel right about it. What if he doesn't like baseball? What if he doesn't like you? As I recall, you liked baseball and your dad couldn't have cared less. Your dad wasn't there for your growing up. Are you planning to be the dad you never had? What if your boy doesn't want you for a dad?"

Ike spoke up, "I feel sorry for the baby. Steven, you're not married. You have to work. You'll never be home. Who is going to raise this child? Strangers?"

Mike piped up, "Do you understand, Steven?"

"No, I don't! I want this baby. I'm the father."

Mike said, "It sounds like your son will be the atonement for your sins. You're ashamed of how you hurt your parents, so this baby will be the perfect child. You'll make sure of it. Your son is the sacrifice for your past, Steven. You'll take your dad's place and you'll be the father you never had. Your baby boy will be the son you never were. Boy, do I feel sorry for the kid, and he's not even born yet."

Someone asked, "What if it's a girl, Steven?"

"It won't be. Believe me, it will be a boy."

As Steven said that, chills ran through me and I prayed, "Oh, God, help Steven."

Ryun and I got a pass to go to his home for dinner. It was a lovely visit. As we entered the house his dad looked concerned for his seventeen-year-old son. There were kids everywhere. Ryun had three brothers and two sisters, eight people in the family to share their love. I enjoyed his parents. They seemed to genuinely love all their children. But Ryun's troubles at home stemmed from no one having had the time to talk to him, and he could never express his anger. Then his buddies pressured him to start smoking pot and drinking.

When we left his house I asked Ryun, "Why do you do it? Don't the drugs and getting drunk scare you?"

"Everyone does it. It's just the thing to do. One time before class I got stoned with a guy who did it all the time, and let me tell you, did I ever hallucinate!"

"What if your hallucinating hadn't stopped? Dr. Meier says that some teenagers come to the hospital who never get over the hallucinations."

"I've thought about that. I don't want to do it any more. I want to be close to my dad. All my friends who smoke and drink come from broken homes."

"So what's your excuse, Ryun? Your home is together. Let's promise each other that when we get out of here, if you have the urge to smoke grass or I am overcome by the monster, I'll think of you and you of me. I'm so glad you're my friend, I don't want you to hurt yourself." We squeezed each other's hands tightly.

Carrie talked about her dad the next day. "I don't want to hurt him. I just want to know that I'm as important as his money."

Mike asked, "What did your dad tell you when you were twelve?"

She said, "I was a slut."

"Were you?"

"No, I didn't even know what a slut was."

"Why did he throw a hibachi at you and chase you with a pole to beat you?"

"I guess I deserved it. Dad always told me never do two things that would embarrass him: get pregnant and commit suicide."

"So why did you choose suicide?" Mike blared out.

"I didn't."

"Oh, come on, Carrie," Mike argued. "You leave home, you starve yourself down to seventy-two pounds, Dr. Minirth tells you you are dying and you say you didn't choose suicide? Who are you really punishing, Carrie?" Carrie wept.

"Why do you always protect your dad?"

"I guess because if he knew he is really a shallow man it would devastate him."

"So you have to be insecure and insignificant and worthless to make him look all powerful, huh?"

"I don't mean to be."

"Huh? Huh?" Mike's huhs really got on my nerves.

Carrie yelled at him, "I don't want to be. I only want to know my dad doesn't regret having me and raising me."

Tab was crying.

"What's going on, Tab?"

In her weak little voice she said, "When I had a stomachache, Dad was concerned; but when the doctors said nothing was physically wrong, Dad said I was nothing but trouble, and he blamed me for my mother's drinking. It made me so mad when he accused me. I would start screaming at him, and when I screamed he would shake me and lock me in the basement."

A bomb was ticking inside me, and it finally exploded. "I don't like your fathers. Your fathers are sick, mean, men. You two are so afraid to ask for their love you rebel by starving yourselves. You are both waiting for Daddy to say, 'I'm so sorry. It was all my fault you starved yourself to death. Don't worry. From now on I will tell you I love you.' Well, let me tell you, it aint going to happen!

"I was lucky. My dad came and said he had failed in a lot of areas, that he was sorry, and that he loved me. But I made a decision even before he came to see me: no more dying for my dad and my family." I was very angry and scared for my two friends.

Tab got out of her chair and threw herself into my arms and cried out, "Oh, God, I hate that man, but I love him. I don't want to die for him. You made me realize I've been so angry I was dying for him."

But Carrie, who had lost fifteen pounds in the hospital and still was afraid of being fat, was curled up in her chair, sobbing, and never heard us.

19

Grand Persons

Sixty days had passed since I'd entered the hospital. One morning I received around forty-five letters from people I had known all my life in Oregon, Oklahoma, Arkansas, and Texas. It was strange to realize I always had those friends but could never reach out to them.

One letter was from my Grandma Hamstreet. That precious neighbor lived next door to us while I was growing up, and I always thought of her as my grandmother. When I went to see her she always had a piece of candy and open arms for me. The tears came as I thought of those sweet moments. Now she was ninety-two years old. She wrote: "My dear, sweet Cyndi, My heart aches that I can't be there with you, but all I can do is pray that God's arms will surround you. Cyndi, I just feel that when you are healed, you will help others. Please know I love you dearly. You will always be my sweet Cyndi."

After I read my mail, Steven came to me with Carrie, and said, "I need to talk to both of you privately." I knew it was something serious. We went into a room and he started crying. He was leaving that day because his insurance had run out and the hospital could no longer keep him.

"Oh, Steven, can't you borrow the money? What about the man who helped you come here?"

"No, I can't ask." His face looked like it had looked the first day I saw him. I realized he had regressed. Last week at the baseball game he was so full of life and laughter, but now he had lost what he'd gained.

Steven said, "I guess I'm like Job and Joseph. God always says no."

"Eventually God said yes to them. Maybe it's you who says no. God wants to have a special relationship with you, a personal one, like father and son, but you make the relationship so hard." I started crying.

The "top three" took each others' hands. "I love you, Cynthia and Carrie," Steven said. His tears started.

"What can I do for you Steven?" I asked.

"I want you, Cynthia, to write your book. I want you to become a public speaker. I want you to allow yourself to marry someone wonderful. But cherish that marriage; don't give so much to others that you lose a marriage.

But Steven was allowed to stay one more day, and my worries about him started vanishing in group therapy.

Steven sat facing the two empty chairs. Mike made him put his mother in one chair and the kind of women he'd had relationships with in the other. He told about his attractions to John Lennon, the peace movement, and women's lib. "Then I ran into Christianity, and I became legalistic. I ended up stuffing everything. You know, I hated my mom's working."

"So," Mike said, "you took it out on the women you went with."

"Yeah, I took it out on women by treating them bad."

Mike was in one of his sarcastic moods. "Right, Mom's not home all of your life, so you find women that care about you and want to take care of you, but you don't want them, so you treat them like dirt, because Mom was never there."

"When I was twelve my parents sent me away to live with an

uncle. I was away from them for two years, and no one told me what was wrong except that Mom was sick. When I was fourteen and back home I started doing dope."

"You really wanted to punish your mother by becoming a doper, so you could get back for all those days she wasn't home, for those two years she left you. But while you were punishing her, you were really punishing yourself," Mike told him.

I reacted. "Steven, you are dying for your mom."

Mike continued. "And isn't it strange that he would like his mom to take care of his baby that's coming? You want your mother to take care of the baby because she didn't take care of you. And the women you fall for don't want your babies. Don't you see that you subconsciously select them so Mom will repent of the way she raised you?"

Then Steven talked about his anger at God. For twenty-nine years he'd been so miserable. "Why, why," he asked, "has God done this to me? I'm not married. No women I love want me."

I took Steven's hands and reminded him that the week before, he had told Carrie and me we were the first women he ever loved or cared about. I told him we loved unconditionally, that he had never rejected me no matter how I looked or felt. "You have always given me a shoulder to cry on. Steven, you say God has always said no. Do you think that he's not listening to you? My friend, when you reached out to me, when you made me happy or told me off because you were angry, God was working through you to help me. And God is loving you through Carrie's and my love for you, and Mike's love for you. He's been working on all of us." I started sobbing. "I have been so angry with God and told him he never listened to me, but you have taught me he has different ways of answering prayers. He told you no. He told us no the days we planned our deaths. We couldn't cope with life, but if God hadn't protected us, we would never have met to share and learn to love. Just think what we would have missed if we were in caskets."

Carrie and I were crying. I began thinking about Grandma Hamstreet. It was spooky, because Carrie was thinking about her grandma, too. When her folks were in college she lived with her grandma. Her grandma hugged her, loved her, was always there to make her feel special, and to soothe her when she was hurting.

Whenever I was lonely while growing up, I'd go next door. Grandma Hamstreet always had a hug and a smile for her "sweet Cyndi." While I was eating candy she would sit down with me and ask, "How is my Cyndi doing?" Now at her age she wrote me to tell me that she still loved me and wished she was there.

"Are you both mourning that love?" Mike asked.

"Yes."

"Why are you sitting there? Comfort each other." We hugged.

Carrie said she moved back to her parents when she was about five and never had love from them like her granny's. She said the first time she met me and we embraced she felt the same kind of love her grandma had given her. I cherished that.

Then Ike started sobbing. He was finally expressing grief. "The only man in my whole life who truly loved me was my grandfather. He always had time to love and accept me. He was so sick at the end. There was nothing I could do. He would raise his arms in that bed for me to hold him, and then one day he died in my arms. My granddad loved me more than my own dad."

Steven was sobbing. "Gramps was there all my life. When I was into drugs I was arrested four times, and it was always Gramps who bailed me out and never criticized me. He loved me, even though I was a junkie. And I never got the chance to say thank you."

Tab was crying. "My granny loved me when I was sick. She'd let me have my fits of anger. She wouldn't lock me up. She would talk to me and bake cookies. My granny loved me."

It was a day I would never forget—Steven, Carrie, Tab, Ike, and I grieving together, remembering those grand people who loved us in spite of ourselves.

Steven was revitalized. His gaunt, dark face was suddenly full of life. He seemed healthy and at peace.

After dinner Steven got the call telling him he was the father of a baby boy. He wouldn't talk to any of us. I stayed up most of the night trying to talk to him, but he would not talk. I read him verses from the Psalms. I didn't know if I could comfort him, but I so much wanted to. He said he wanted to be alone.

When I finally got to bed my sleep was peaceful for the first time since I'd entered the hospital. I dreamed I was a public speaker, talking about the love of God.

Lord, would you please keep healing me and let me serve you?

At breakfast, Steven sat eating those awful hospital eggs. I was sad thinking that the next morning he would not be there. He took my hand and said, "Look at it this way; at least I won't have to eat these crazy eggs. Maybe I'll go to a neat restaurant and have eggs Benedict." That didn't help much.

After breakfast he asked Carrie and me to go to the office with him. The decision was made: he was giving up the baby for adoption. None of us talked on the way downstairs; even our breathing seemed to cease. I signed, Carrie signed, and the papers were notarized. Steven's baby boy would be given to some unknown parents who wanted a child. I prayed that God would find the right home for him. Tears came to Steven's eyes. I reached for his and Carrie's hands and we walked back upstairs.

It was time to say good-bye. I was sad at Steven's leaving, but so happy he'd found some peace. He would be locked in my soul forever.

Before he left we exchanged letters. He told me of his love for me and the special place I had in his life. I told him of what his acceptance and love had meant to me. He had taught me much, and our friendship and God's love would see us through anything.

20

More Friends

The group felt good about Steven when we met the next day.

Carrie, too, had a new sense of hope. Her dad and brother had surprised her by coming to see her. Her brother had totaled her car, but he was not hurt. She didn't care about the car, but was puzzled by her dad. Any other time he would have been furious and only concerned about the car, but now he showed love and concern for his son. Carrie said he no longer acted like he was on a throne.

"He really does love us." she said. "I got the car in place of my dad's love. I loved that car, but now that it's totaled, I don't care if I have to ride a bike the rest of my life. The fact that my dad is concerned about my brother and says things are going to change is what matters."

My friend Jessica, the one I always thought had it all together, was coming to visit. My anger toward her had subsided. Looking back, I realized she did try to help me. She would try to get me to go out with her when she knew something was bothering me, but I wouldn't go. I did not want to be with this girl who had everything going for her, because if she found out about the real me she would reject me.

I remembered the high I would get from binging. I would walk to a restaurant next to the TV station thinking, "Oh, I get to eat and eat and eat and then get rid of it and not gain weight!" I'd claim the three roast beef sandwiches and three pieces of pie were for my TV crew. After my usual routine in the rest room, Jessica would try to talk to me, try to get me to spend the weekend with her or go to a party. I would say I was too busy. And I remembered she often called me to see how I was. She did try, but I refused her help.

I was in the lobby when Jessica arrived. We looked at each other, started crying, and embraced. "I need you, Jessica."

"Oh, Cynthia, I've always needed you. You're the best friend I've ever had. Please forgive me for not knowing what to do."

"Forgive me for not opening up to you. But you couldn't have helped me; no one could. I was too sick for anyone to reach me."

Our friendship was renewed. Yet, I knew it would be different from now on. She wanted me to hurry back to work. I told her I wasn't sure if I could go back to being in television. I told her I had to do something about the monster in others. If I had suffered from it all those years and told no one, then there must be thousands of other women just like me.

Jessica looked doubtful. She thought I belonged in the newsroom. But deep inside I knew someone was telling me that I would never go back to the TV reporter's life.

Ryun and I played miniature golf. I had never played before. Ryun was opening new horizons of fun to me, and he was an expert at it. He was becoming a best friend. His parents had me over for dinner— nine people at one table. They said they fell in love thinking they would have only two children, but six arrived.

After dinner we played tennis, then got to talking about Carrie.

Ryun said she was the kind of girl he was always attracted to. I wondered why. "I guess it's because she needs to be taken care of."

I couldn't understand that. "Carrie is so insecure. She is beautiful, but you can tell her that time and time again, and she won't believe you. Why are guys attracted to someone who is so dependent? Look at it this way. I'll bet every girl you have liked was a Carrie who wanted to be taken care of, used you, and dropped you like a hot potato. Am I correct?"

"Yeah."

"And I'll bet every girl who needed to be taken care of never expressed her liking for you, or that you were her friend first of all and she cared about you no matter what. And I'll bet every girl you liked who needed to be taken care of never did anything kind to you. It was always you doing the giving. Am I right?"

"Yeah."

"I think it would be boring to have someone you constantly have to coax and say, 'Oh, Carrie, you're pretty,' and she constantly says, 'Oh, I'm not.' I just feel that people, myself included, have got to take care of themselves first. Yes, people need people, but not to feed off other people. And that's the end of my heavy speech."

"You're right. I never thought about it."

"Ryun, I don't want you to develop a pattern with women like I did with men."

When we got back we went to the day room. It was late, and everyone had gone to bed or was out on pass. But Carrie was up, crying and puffy eyed. She had binged and felt guilty. She had lost weight that week and was trying to gain it back in one night. I was upset with her. "Carrie, don't you realize how attractive you are to guys? When are you giving up the control your body has on you, and realize that you are OK? You don't have to be a pitiful case to get a guy." Carrie wouldn't say anything. "I'm tired of talking to you, Carrie. Only you can learn to love yourself."

When I went to bed I felt guilty for having said those things to her. But I was so tired of telling her the truth and her not believing it. I prayed, "God, please help Carrie. I can't reach her."

In the group session the next day, everything broke loose. Ryun had stayed up with Carrie all night talking to her. One staff member started on Carrie. "I think, no I don't think, I know, you love to seduce men. Oh, you can put on this act. You play this game that you're coy, they are attracted to you, and you let them think you like them. When they really start caring about you, you slam the door in their faces."

Then an aide said, "I wonder if you seduced your best friend that raped you."

I became angry over that statement. "Nobody has the right to do that to any woman. I don't care if the woman seduces him, no one has the right to attack her. Carrie did not ask for the rape. The guy forced her out of the car and raped her."

Carrie became hysterical. "No, no, it wasn't my fault."

"It wasn't? Why didn't your dad comfort you? Why didn't you tell someone you had been raped?" the aide asked. "Come on, Carrie, admit it. You seduced the guy."

"No, I didn't, I didn't." Carrie's chest was heaving. She could barely talk through her sobs. "It wasn't my fault. He was my best friend. He had never touched me. He got me drunk that night. I tried so hard to make him stop, but I couldn't stop him. The rape was not my fault!"

Carrie finally said it: the rape was not her fault. The seduction accusation was a setup. The staff wanted Carrie to admit from her innermost being that it wasn't her fault. They were trying to make her realize that she punished guys by letting them come to within a certain distance of her and then dropped them, acting like she cared when she really couldn't stand them. She hadn't meant to do that, but she couldn't help it.

Carrie got a rubber bat and hit and hit the rapist. Then she used the punching bag. She finally released her anger.

Later, she came to my room and we embraced. She sobbed and told me she was sorry. "But, Cynthia, it's so hard to believe I'm OK."

"I know, I know."

21

Woman to Woman

I dreaded the session with Mom. I was terrified of what I might learn. She told me later she was terrified, too. She arrived looking beautiful, and we went into Mike's office. He asked me what I wanted to talk about.

I asked why she didn't say anything when Dad had been there for the previous sessions. "I don't know. I was hurt. You and Dad usually do all the talking, so I guess I didn't have anything to say."

"Mother, that makes me so angry. What do you mean, we do all the talking? You know you have the right to say what's on your mind."

"I guess I feel it doesn't matter what I say."

"But it does. Mom, are you jealous of me?"

She retorted, "No! Why would you ask such a thing? I've always been proud of you; I couldn't have asked for a better daughter."

My little girl suddenly became angry. "Mom, why were you always sick when I was growing up?"

"I wasn't that sick all the time. You have that out of proportion."

"You were, too. You were always in the hospital, or in bed when I came home from school. Oh, poor Mom; I'm tired of hearing about it. Why couldn't you stand on your own two feet and do something? After my divorce, you went to bed, you were so depressed. I needed you; I was the one that was divorced, but where were you?"

Mom was breaking. I didn't want to hurt her, but the anger was so intense. "I'm sorry I wasn't there for you, Cyndi. I guess I didn't know you needed me. You were always a miniature adult when you were growing up. You didn't know how poor we were. Dad had to be on the road for the school, and I worked part-time. A couple years I went to school. We always had students staying with us and Robby was in trouble. So I guess, like your bulimia, my illness was my escape—sleeping and getting ulcers because I couldn't handle my loneliness."

"I'm angry about something else. The last two years I have been telling you about my bulimia. I told you I wanted to die, and you would comment, 'Don't talk that way. You know how that would hurt your dad and me.'"

Mom said vehemently, "You know, I'm tired of your blaming your dad and me for everything. What about us? Our parents made a lot of mistakes, but I don't blame them for my problems."

That comment really made me angry. I yelled, "Don't you understand, Mother? You have never been desperate like me. I wanted to put a gun to my head. Even now in the hospital, I would sometimes kill myself if I had a gun. I've wanted to die. Mother, it is somebody's fault, and yes, in many ways, it's your and Dad's fault. I have to find reasons for this self-destructiveness, or I won't make it. But I will forgive."

Mike said, "Close your eyes, Cynthia." I shut my eyes. He told me to relax and let thoughts and memories come to my mind. "Let's talk to the little girl. What happened to that little girl?"

Oh, no, the hot water. "Mom and Dad, where are you? Those three big men and three women in the white suits are ripping my skin where I go to the bathroom, Momma. Why are they hurting me? The nurse told me to shut up."

The scene changed. I was about eight and in my room eating five candy bars. Momma had given me a quarter. Those memories of eating candy in the room where I played make-believe were pleasant. But this time I was crying and lonely. No one was there to talk to me or hold me. Then I heard Robby screaming, Mom crying and Dad yelling. No one saw that I couldn't bear the pain.

Once when I couldn't take it, I ran out of the house, sat down in the dirt under a tree, and cried and cried. I went back into the house, and no one ever knew I had left. I rocked myself to sleep. Then, when I was twelve, I stopped crying. Crying was not worth it. Nobody cared.

While I was reliving this, I heard sobs and felt arms around me. When I opened my eyes, I was drained. Mom was holding me, saying, "I'm so sorry, so sorry. We were ignorant and didn't know what you were going through."

"Momma, I didn't know what I was going through, either. You and Dad did the best you could. In my eyes you were the perfect parents. I never wanted to hurt you, please believe that; but I have to find out why I was dying. And yes, you and Dad were to blame, but you didn't know. I didn't understand myself what was happening within me. Mom, I love you; I'd do anything for you."

Mom and I were still embracing. Any jealousy we may have had of each other was now irrelevant. I realized that she'd had her own pain and suffering to bear, and I hadn't known about it, just as she hadn't known mine.

"I don't know, Mom, but you're probably okay now because you've had Dad at home the past eleven years. I have no one."

Mike shot out, "And do you suppose that's your answer, to find a husband to spend your life with?"

Sarcastically I said, "Well, suppose it is?" I started shaking. Yes, I would like to get married and have a family, but the word marriage made me freeze. Who would want me?

Daddy surprised us by being at the hotel when we got there. My sleep that night was frightening, with the little girl haunting me, my body shaking and twitching, crying. Mom held me and rubbed my head. She said I was like a little baby all through the night.

Mom left in the morning, but Dad had business in Dallas, so we spent most of the day together. It was a day of revelations.

We went to the Old West town in Fort Worth. We had our pictures taken in one of those photo shops where you dress up in Old Western clothes. Dad dressed as a preacher and I as a saloon girl. After the picture was developed, Dad could not believe how much we looked alike. I always knew, but after twenty-eight years Dad realized it for the first time. We had the same expression, and our noses and mouths were alike. "Now that I'm twenty-eight," I thought, "my dad may finally start noticing me."

Throughout the day we talked. I asked him if, while I was growing up and he was traveling, he didn't once think I needed him. "No, I really didn't. I just knew you had my love, and I was there in spirit."

"We learn too late, huh, Dad?"

"Yes, we do. You don't know how many times I have kicked myself and grieved over Robby. I realize now all his rebellion was simply his crying out for help."

Toward the end of the day I began to feel tired and sick, and asked Dad to take me back to the hospital. I wondered if I would ever feel strong and healthy.

When it was time to say good-bye I broke down. Dad held me and told me it was okay. "I'll always be here for you, Cyndi."

I thought back to when I landed my first TV job. He was going off somewhere again, and when I said a tearful good-bye he acted cold, as if to say, "Buck up, girl. You're on your own and you can do it. Don't depend on anyone else."

But this scene was different. He was now telling me I could depend on him. Why do we learn too late?

My night was filled with dreams of caskets, and I was in them. I awoke drained.

In the group it hit me that I felt guilty for being sick, and ashamed for hurting my parents.

Mike said, "You're not guilty; you don't *have* to be perfect. You have a built-in self-hate button, a 'you're-no-good Cynthia' button."

"But I do feel badly. I didn't mean to get sick."

"Then tell us, 'I didn't mean to get sick, but it's okay that I did, because my little girl perceived things the wrong way, and my family dynamics made me that way.'"

I said, "I'm not perfect, and it's okay I got sick, but now I will get well."

I told the group about the time my dad and I spent together, and about another conversation of the day before. I said I might become a public speaker on bulimia and maybe write a book. He said, "No, Cyndi, let's not do anything in haste. You're not Pat Boone's daughter."

That made me angry. I looked at him and said, "But I'm a King's kid, God's child, and if he wants me to do it, it will happen. Who can argue with God?"

The group laughed. Mike said, "It might be rough. Maybe your family has room for only one public speaker and author." My dad was both.

"Well, then, tough cookies, but I'll do what I need to do."

Tab was shivering and crying. She wished she could talk to her dad the way I could. "I'm scared of going home. I'm so lonely at home, especially at night. There were so many times I couldn't sleep and wanted to talk to someone, so I'd go into my parents' room. My dad would get mad and tell me not to be so stupid. 'Don't be a mouse. Go to bed and leave your mother and me alone. You are so silly.'"

I remembered when I was young and in bed and afraid. The blinds showed shadows from outside the window, and they looked like monsters. I just knew the "buger-bear" out there was going to kill me, but I couldn't yell out, I was so frightened. So I just lay there and shook and cried.

"You didn't want to bother anyone, huh, Cynthia?" good old Mike said. "Well, you two, get up and comfort each other for all those nights you were so lonely." Tab and I hugged.

Anna, Carrie, and I were talking about men. We wanted men in our lives, but we always went for the wrong ones or never allowed wonderful men into our lives. Carrie felt she didn't deserve anyone good. Anna thought after her husband's death she'd never find another man like him. Her second marriage was failing because she kept comparing the two.

Carrie told about a wonderful guy who once entered her life. He was a good, solid Christian. He loved her, but because she felt unacceptable to him, she dropped him.

Mike said, "You three ladies are all alike. Cynthia's monster is really her little girl slamming the door shut tight in everyone's face, and that little girl is saying, 'Stay away from me, I'm no good, I'm damaged freight. If Mommy and Daddy weren't there when I was burned and scarred, then I must be bad, so good guys, stay away from me.'" Mike was acting out my little girl to a T.

The idea hit me with new impact. There hadn't exactly been a monster trying to destroy me all those years, but my little girl—that little girl who was burned and "died" when she was four years old. Yet, she came to haunt me all those years, whispering, "Go ahead and destroy yourself."

Then Mike said, "It's time to merge the little girl with the gorilla. You'll become a woman, Cynthia."

I didn't know what to expect when, in our next session, Mike made me sit in the chair. First I was Cyrilla the gorilla. I hated that. I didn't want to be a gorilla.

Cyrilla looked at the little girl in the other chair. "Now, look, little girl, I'm tired of being so strong and independent and needless. Do you realize being strong really is a weakness?" Mike made me switch chairs.

The little girl spoke up. "But we've got to be strong and protect ourselves from everyone. We've been trying so hard to destroy Cynthia, why should we quit?" Switch chairs.

Cyrilla said, "Because Cynthia has had enough heartache and loneliness. This being a tough girl is good for nothing. She is fighting with us to become whole, and I'm getting tired of struggling with her." Switch.

The little girl cried, "But I've been sad and lonely for so long, angry and always getting hurt. I don't know if I can let it go." Switch.

"You know, little girl, your mom and dad were *really* out in the waiting room when we were burned. They did love us, they did! Little girl, you need to come alive in the woman Cynthia. You need to show your feelings of delight and happiness. You need to be curious and adventurous. It's time to combine the qualities of the little girl with the qualities of being a woman." Switch.

The little girl cried, "But I'm so scared of becoming a woman. I may get hurt."

The gorilla said, "We may get hurt, but at least we know what we've been doing all these years, trying to be Robby's savior and the son of the family. It's time to free ourselves from all the bitterness and pain. It's time to forgive, and start living for God through Cynthia, the woman. I don't want to be Cyrilla any longer. I want to be Cynthia. I want to be more dependent on people. I want to become more feminine. Let's merge."

Mike said, "Okay, Cyrilla, close your eyes and picture the gorilla packing her bags and going away forever. Picture Cynthia, the woman, strong, yes, but healthily dependent, giving, with lots of love and open arms to receive the gifts that others bring her." Switch.

"Okay, little girl," Mike said, "close your eyes." The little girl shivered. "Now remember all those lonely times in bed, all those monsters, the days of self-destruction. Put them all in a suitcase and ship them off, never to return. Now picture the little girl, playfully mischievous, in the woman Cynthia, who has a smile and hug to offer, the little girl who flirts with guys and can giggle. Vanish all thoughts of slamming the door. Picture the little girl in the woman knocking on the doors of people who are good and wholesome and who will love and accept the woman Cynthia, no matter what.

"Now switch to the third chair," Mike said, "and picture this new woman Cynthia. Cyrilla and the little girl have merged their positive traits in the woman."

At that moment something happened. I felt whole, at one with myself.

"Now, Cynthia, look at everyone in this room and say, 'Hello, I'm Cynthia, a whole new woman, who cares, and loves, and desires to receive love.'"

"Carrie," I said, "I, Cynthia, love and receive love. May I give you a hug? Hey, Ike," I batted by eyes, mocking Mae West, "how'd you like to come up to my place sometime?" We hugged and laughed. I felt great. "Oh, Sam, hello. I'm Cynthia, the real woman."

I can feel, cry, love. Good-bye, sad little girl; good-bye Cyrilla. Hello, Cynthia. Watch out, world, because here comes Cynthia Joye Rowland. Emerging. Oh, I like that word!

22

Getting There

Seventy days I'd been in the hospital. I was beginning to have a sense of peace.

All my pain had come to the surface and my soul was saying, "It's time to forgive the past and start connecting with the future. I want my soul, mind and heart to be one."

In the mail I received from my mom a package containing a blouse, some pajamas, and a stuffed gorilla.

Mom had sent me a Cyrilla! Thanks, Mom, thanks. She was trying to get me to laugh at myself in a healthy way. I loved that little lady. It was sad that the majority of patients never heard from their families, and were lonely when they received nothing at mail time.

God, thank you for my mom and dad.

Ryun left the hospital that day. My sweet friend was getting along great with his dad, doing lots of things with him. Ryun was like a new person. He had always been there for me, touching me with his warmth, smiles, and encouragement. Now another friend was leaving me, and it hurt. But I had to accept this part of life, that nothing is forever. However, I could always cherish the memories.

Elizabeth had been discharged from the hospital, and a few evenings later we went out to eat. After I returned I found some cookies Sam had brought into the day room, and I ate twelve of them. I made myself sick. There were twenty people in the room; why didn't I scream out for help? Carrie was nearby and I didn't say a thing to her.

I had to talk to someone after I ate. The nurses said they were too busy. I thought about Tab and knew she'd understand; therefore, I went to her door. She was already under the covers, but she told me to come on in.

"Tab, I didn't want to do it, but I lost control. I ate twelve cookies and now I feel so guilty."

"Twelve. Oh, I know how you feel. That's why I don't eat a bit. I'm afraid of losing control. Last night I ate two pieces of carrot cake when I wasn't even hungry."

"Yes, but you need to gain weight."

Stubbornly, little seventy-pound Tab said, "That is not the point, Cynthia. I should have had only one piece of cake. Why did you do it?"

"I don't know. Something is going on inside me and I don't know what."

"You know what I think, Cynthia? I think Elizabeth frustrated you. You're always so concerned about her and the others that you don't think about your own needs."

"So what are my needs, Tab? Why did I have to eat? I don't know what I need before a binge. I'm scared, Tab. It would be easy to starve myself tomorrow, or go back to being bulimic. I'm still afraid of getting fat."

"Okay," said Tab. "You've binged, but tomorrow is a new day. You feel guilty now, but we will start tomorrow together. You'll eat breakfast and eat right. And if I see you eating snacks, I'm going to stop you and ask what is wrong."

"Tab, why do you love me?"

"You care about me. I can go to you and you listen and never put me down."

"I love you for all those reasons, too, Tab."

As I got into bed I thought about my evening with Elizabeth. It was true. When we were together we always talked only about her. Something else bothered me that I hadn't realized before: she constantly talked about food, restaurants, ice cream and candy. That frightened me. Elizabeth had lost weight but she talked about food all the time. If Elizabeth regressed after leaving the hospital, would I when I left?

My nightmares were filled with food and laxatives. I felt like a slave to food and pills. I thought maybe if the staff put me in a strait jacket it would stop my binging.

When I got up, my face was swollen. I told Dr. Gutierrez about my guilt. He said, "The guilt could override the reasons you binged. What was going on before the binge? Was it Ryun leaving?"

"Maybe. But I think it was being frustrated over Elizabeth's not listening to me. She also hated my haircut. It scares me."

"It?"

"The click in my brain, a wall going up, the urge to self-destruct, the little girl slamming the door."

Dr. Gutierrez said, "Whatever happened built up, and instead of dealing with it, you suppressed it. You have got to stop this pattern. You must deal with your emotions."

"The sadness and frustration hit me last night," I said. "Elizabeth and I both have eating disorders. We were sitting in a restaurant and the meal was coming. I had told Elizabeth she had to order a high-calorie meal because she had not eaten all day. Before the meal arrived, terror was written all over her face. She was calculating the calories of her hamburger. I asked her what was wrong, and she said nothing. But I knew she was thinking, 'Oh, all those calories. I'm going to get fat.' I didn't enjoy my meal but ate past my full point. Then I felt guilty for eating at all, afraid I might regress like Elizabeth. So I ate twelve cookies. I became even more scared. Will I become bulimic again when I get out?"

I asked the group, "Can you see when I put up a wall around myself?"

"Yes, and you look scary."

"Carrie, are you scared of me?"

"Yes, I wanted to come over last night and talk to you, but the look on your face scared me, the look that says, 'Stay back.'"

"That was to keep you from knowing how disgusting I was," I said. "I was afraid you would see me sneaking those cookies and I was ashamed. Please, people, if you see my wall coming up, don't be afraid to break through it."

Later, I went to a movie by myself. Loneliness engulfed me, just as it used to. I rushed back to the hospital to be with people, to the warmth of people.

Early Sunday morning I got up and ran for the first time since my admission. My legs felt wonderful, and I pushed myself. I wanted this to become a healthy habit instead of an obsession. I thought of all the mornings I had taken laxatives on an empty stomach and had run four miles. I remembered feeling weak but thinking I had to lose weight. It's a wonder my heart didn't stop during those weird times. But this day the running felt good. Maybe I was on my way to health. I was happy to be alive.

At church I made an effort to be friendly. A girl introduced herself and asked me out to lunch, but the old lonely Cynthia said no.

I was looking around in church, and suddenly the sight of a young man made my stomach churn. He was David Snow, Matthew's best man at our wedding. I had last seen him seven years before, when I was a reporter. Now he had a little boy sitting on his knee, and a beautiful wife.

After church I went to him. He was amazed to see me. His family happened to be visiting the church, having recently moved to Dallas from California.

I told David what I had learned two weeks before about Matthew. He said, "Cynthia, Matthew had three or four lives we didn't know about. You're lucky it was over in four months instead of forty years and four kids later." David and his wife asked me to come over for dinner soon, and I told them I would.

I went back to my room and slept until three. I was exhausted and wondered if I would ever feel healthy.

In group therapy Tab was upset. She and her mom had become closer. She did not want to see her dad, but the army man had arrived from his mission two days early.

There were no hugs, and he didn't ask her how she was. I asked her if that didn't make her angry.

"No, but he did bring me a flower from Hawaii. I don't think it was because he wanted to, but because he had to make himself look okay. But my mom and I hugged each other this week, and we haven't done that in years. We talked and laughed. Then he had to come home and he wouldn't let me talk to her alone."

My new roommate, Penny, was crying, and I went to her to hold her. She sobbed, "I hate feeling bad all the time, and I don't understand."

"Keep crying," I said. "You've got to get that anger, fear, and sadness out, because that is the way to get well." It felt good to reach out and comfort her. "Believe me, Penny, I know."

Her mascara ran all over my white blouse, which made her worry. "So what? Stains are not important. Soothing your pain is what matters to me."

Dear God, it feels so right to care, to reach out and feel another's heartache. I know there is hope that you do heal us.

Dr. Gutierrez told me I could leave in two weeks. The thought scared me, but I could honestly tell him I was figuring things out. To think, I would be leaving my cocoon in two weeks!

23

Down to the Last Week

Mike laid some heavy stuff on me. "First of all, I want you to come to the group tomorrow looking younger than you are.

"Secondly, I want you to write a paper on how to court a man, and another paper titled, 'What I Need From People.' Three assignments by tomorrow."

Panic. Dress younger than I was? What did that mean? I went to Carrie and Tab. They said, "You always wear suits. You always look authoritative. Mike obviously wants you to look more feminine." It was true; I always wore suits. I wore them to work so I would look slimmer, and they would cover my stomach if I binged.

My mom came to visit, and we went shopping for a new dress. I found one with polka dots, and a big ribbon around the waist.

Then I worked on my papers. In "What I Need From People" I said I needed acceptance, openness, love, hugs, encouragement, honesty, faithfulness, help in growing, counsel, and help in overcoming my loneliness.

In "How to Court" a Man I wrote that, once I found one I was attracted to, I would make a slow genuine effort to show my interest by being friendly, maybe do some "eye killing" (Marta taught me that one), invite him to take me to breakfast or lunch (that's safe), and slowly open up about myself. I'd want to have fun, doing non-serious things at first. I would be interested in his work, hobbies, family and future. I'd make him feel big by encouraging him, listening to him, and being there when he needed me. I'd want to be myself with him.

I added: "P.S. Mike, I don't think I can handle dating. I haven't done it in so long, it scares me. And when you mention marriage, I shudder."

Ike's time for discharge came, and he was making plans to go to college in the fall. His parents were getting a divorce, but, surprisingly, it didn't bother him as the prospect of it had for so long. He was relieved they were being honest with him and with each other. His mother had arthritis and his father had been unfaithful. Ike was greatly concerned for his mother, fearing he would have to take care of her, but now she said she did not expect him to do so because she could manage.

When it was time for Ike to leave I was sorry to see him go. The young man had taught me much. We had been genuine friends, both of us having had to learn to have friends of the opposite sex without sexual implications. Everyone was in the hall hugging and saying good-bye. He looked at me to say the last good-bye.

"Ike, I love you," I said.

Big handsome Ike took me in his strong arms and we held each other tightly. "Cynthia, you have taught and given me much. You are a beautiful lady who has much to offer this world. And remember, whenever you get down, that I love you." Tears were streaming down the giant's face. "I'm going to call you next week and we're going out on a date."

Tab was sitting in the hot seat. She didn't know what to talk about, so Mike said, "Go back as far as you can."

Tab started quivering and crying."I see me as an infant, and my dad's picture is setting on a shelf." She talked of her dad's coming and going through the years, but never giving her attention. "I want my daddy to love me," she cried.

"You're not dead, yet," Mike said when Tab opened her eyes.

"I know. I guess I made it this far without him. I can continue to make it even if he won't give me love, right?" She stopped crying and looked at me. "I'm going to make it whether I have him or not. I have made it this far, and I'm sixteen." Tiny Tabitha turned into a determined woman.

Carrie got in the chair. Her self-worthlessness was alive, mean and strong. Everyone in the room looked at her and said, "You are worthy, Carrie." She didn't believe us. Mike told her to look at everyone and say, "I am worthy." She couldn't do it; therefore, she just cried and left the room.

I don't know what got into me, but I sat in the chair and told Mike I wanted a sense of humor, to be able to laugh at myself and at life when it got too serious.

"Okay, sit in that chair and laugh."

It was weird. I started giggling and laughing hysterically. Everyone started laughing with me, but we didn't know what we were laughing about. It was good to rip and roar with everyone.

After the hilarity was over, Mike looked at me and said, "When you walk out the door you will think of jokes, and laugh all afternoon." I didn't believe him, but as I walked out the door with Tab, I started laughing and couldn't stop. Tears rolled down my face because I was laughing so hard. Tab started laughing hysterically with me. We passed the nurses' station, trying to hold back our laughter, but it broke out all over again. I looked back at Mike, and he was grinning from ear to ear. I don't know what he did to me, but our laughter was right that day.

David Snow and his wife had me over for dinner. It was a pleasant evening. He was a stockbroker. I enjoyed being with him and his kind wife.

I told her about my bulimia, and she said, "Cynthia, you should become a spokeswoman for people with this disorder." Was God trying to tell me something?

I was telling the group I was glad I had been born, when Carrie started again on being unworthy and wishing she hadn't been born. I tried to remind her that she was making progress communicating with her parents, her father showed some signs of loving his children, guys liked her, and I loved her.

Mike tried to show her it was like slapping her friends in the face when she rejected their love and support. He was slapping himself in the face saying, "You're the victim. You love the role."

She got angry and yelled at him to stop, then said she didn't have the right to be angry. I wondered how anyone could ever help her.

I had a visit from Ryun a week before I was to leave. He was strangely distant. His attitude bothered me. "What is it, Ryun?"

"Nothing. I'm just in a mellow mood."

I began to think Ryun wished I wasn't there. "What is going on, Ryun?"

"Oh, I don't know. I've decided I really don't want to spend any more time with you."

"Okay, I understand that, but you didn't feel this way a few weeks ago."

"You're always so available."

"But isn't that what friends are for?" Something was not right about this whole situation. "If you aren't available for your friends, then what's friendship all about?" I was hurt and angry. "This always happens to me. What have I done?"

Ryun looked away. "The truth is, I smoked grass today," he said.

"You what? You jerk! You promised you would never do that

again, that you would tell me if you were tempted. Your parents spent all that money for you to get over drugs, and what do you do? You stab them and everyone else in the back. You jerk!" My tears stung. "What if I had binged today and went to the drugstore to pop laxatives, how would you feel?"

Fear ran deep inside me. My friend had been out of the hospital two weeks and had gone back to being the old Ryun. I was leaving the hospital in six days. Would I regress too?

Ryun was crying. He told me he had gone to lunch with a guy from work who asked him to smoke with him, and "I did."

"Ryun, you have to stand up for what is right. Who knows, you may have prevented that man from smoking if you had said no."

We both cried. "I swear, Cynthia, I will never smoke grass again." Ryun left. Our friendship would never be quite the same again.

It was past midnight. I had planned to spend the night at my roommate's house. I drove to the house and went to the door. The key she had given me did not fit. Dogs barked inside the house. I froze, my body literally paralyzed. She hadn't told me about the dogs. I walked back to the street. The number was right (but I was on the wrong street, I found out later). I was so frightened . . . I was so alone . . . I was so tired. I crawled into the back seat of my car to sleep and grieved all night. I told myself, *I don't need anyone.* But my hot tears were telling me I was lying.

At daybreak I drove back to the hospital, too hurt and embarrassed to tell the staff what had happened. I crawled into bed, my throat was sore, and after whimpering about my sorry state, I fell asleep.

At nine I got up and went into the day room for breakfast. Since it was Sunday, most of the patients were either sleeping or out on pass. There were breakfast trays everywhere. The little girl inside me said, "Go ahead, destroy yourself. You're no good. Look, you're losing another friend again, so go ahead and destroy yourself."

I did. I ate five boxes of cereal, two plates of eggs and four rolls. Panic gripped me. I ran to my bathroom to throw up. I turned on the water so the staff could not hear me. No one had seen me in the day room. Okay, Ryun, if you can smoke pot, then I can vomit!" I was purged, then sick. I went to bed and cried myself to sleep.

I got up at five that evening. Rachel was on duty and I told her what I had done.

"Why didn't you come to us before the binge?" she asked.

"I couldn't. I didn't know how to. Well, I wouldn't!"

God, I can't go back to that horrid addiction. I've been here almost three months. I will die if I go back to that monster.

Please help me.

On top of all that, a good friend from college, with whom I'd kept contact through the years, called me later Sunday evening from Arizona where she lived. She knew about my bulimia and had an idea how sick I was.

She told me she and her husband were expecting a baby in a month. I was crushed she hadn't told me the joyful news sooner. But I knew she'd been afraid to tell me for fear I would feel sorry for myself, since I had no joyful news to give her.

Mike noticed how bad I looked the next morning. "Have I been that sick, that my best friend couldn't share good news with me?" I cried. Then I told him that Ryun rejected my friendship and that I'd regressed by binging and purging.

"You will also regress when you leave," he said. "But regression means growth."

"Regression means agony!"

"No, regression means you will think about why you regressed, then you will change. You have to think before you eat. When you get the urge to binge and purge, it means you need people. You have to start on people binges, Cynthia. You need people."

Sam and Carrie watched me in group therapy. They could see something was wrong. Carrie did not know what to do, so she left the room. I talked to Sam about Ryun. "Sam, it hurts to see Ryun regress and smoke pot again. It hurt the other day when Carrie said, 'I want to feel, but not as much as Cynthia.'"

Wise Sam said, "You have the capacity to care so deeply that you are overwhelmed by your feelings and perceptions. You have a gift to perceive what others are going through. Use your perceptions as a blessing. I am sure you will help others when you get out of this hospital. With that gift you can really minister to other bulimics. You could walk into any audience and speak to their hearts right where they sat. You would know what they needed to hear.

"I think Ryun is scared," Sam continued. "He wanted to hurt you, and I think you need to find out why. The ending of that friendship hurt you deeply."

"Sam, I really care about his family. Do you think his mom and dad would talk to me?"

"Yes."

Ryun's parents did want to see me. "I want you to know you and your family mean a lot to me," I said when I got to their house. "Ryun and I have shared a lot of pain and have grown together."

"We know," his mom said, "and we are grateful to you. Ryun has been a different kid since you came into his life. We know you tell him he's lucky to have his family, and he acts differently toward us whenever he talks with you. He's scared. He knows you are leaving Dallas soon so he decided to shut you out of his life early. That keeps him from hurting when you say good-bye."

"So that's it," I said. "I may not see him for a long time, but we can keep in touch over the mail and encourage each other."

His parents told me that Ryun could not handle inner pain. When other friends had moved away, he never kept in touch, because, as his mom put it, "It hurts too bad."

I said, "If he were twenty-eight, I'd have a diamond ring on my finger."

"Yes, we know," and we all laughed. We talked about the drug problem. His parents said, "We can't stop Ryun. He will have to be the one to stop."

Ryun's mom said, "Cynthia, there is something I'd like to share with you. I love my husband and family, all seven of them. But tomorrow the house might blow away or catch fire and my family

killed, and I'd be all alone. So I have learned that the only assurance
I have is God and his Son, Jesus Christ. He is my basis for living. I
depend totally on him, because if I put all my dependence on my
family, and tomorrow I lost them, where would I be? Don't depend
on people, but put your trust in God, Cynthia."

All my life I had heard, "Don't put your trust in people, but in the
Lord." Now I heard it again and understood. All those years I had
depended on one person or on my career to fulfill me, and ended
up empty. But God is the only source that can fill my life. Something
happened to me in that moment. I had a real revelation: Jesus was
already my Lord, but he could also be an intimate friend who would
fill my void.

I loved Ryun's parents. They were good people who believed in
God. Ryun was lucky to have them.

Ike and I went out to eat that evening, and it was wonderful to see
him. He had been doing great. I told him about Ryun. "But what are
you doing for yourself?" he asked.

"Ike, I've learned I need a lot of people, people who will accept
me, like you. I have to keep trying not to back away from people,
and not give up. If one person doesn't want my love, I'm just going
to go on to the next person."

"That's the way to do it, Cynthia."

I went back to the hospital feeling wonderful.

I drove to the store where Ryun worked. When I walked in, he
looked at me strangely. This was not the sweet Ryun of old. He
looked like the shell of someone else living inside him.

"Ryun," I said, "I know you're hurting and scared. So am I, but I
am concerned about you anyway, and will never stop wanting the
best for your life, no matter what."

His mouth sort of dropped open. He didn't know what to say or
do. So I said, "See ya later. I've gotta go." I thought to myself as I was
leaving, "Well, one person can give me a drop, another may fill my

cup half full, but what does it matter? Each human being can give me something." That and my intimacy with God would sustain me.

Back at the hospital, I ran to Sam and Carrie. "I'm making it," I told them. I was running to people who loved me, learning not to give up when someone rejected me. Ryun had the problem, not me. I would not give up on him nor on my other friends just because he had rejected me. "I'm not going to be afraid to love any longer. And if I feel, I feel. I'm not going to love only one person, but fifty people, a hundred people, each in a different way." Sam and Carrie rejoiced with me.

I would be leaving in two days, and I knew I was going to be okay!

God, please forgive me. I regressed. I was beginning to look for the one person again. Accept my forgiveness of my dad. He was doing the best he knew how. Thank you for what you have taught me. Help me to reach out to those who will give back. But God, protect me when I find people who don't want me or treat me badly. Help me to run to those who love me, no matter what. Most of all, help me to always find refuge in your love.

24

Hello, World!

It was Sam's day to leave. The man whose volcano of anger once erupted because of me had become a father figure, my friend.

Tab was emotional about his leaving and about my leaving in two days. "You're my family, Sam, the dad I never had, Cynthia the sister I never had, the best friend I never had. But now my family is breaking up."

I had new strength. "You know, Tab, nothing remains forever. But we are well. We have found love for the first time. We know we'll never forget each other. I had a letter from Steven today, and he said the memories of us here are keeping him going. We will have to hang on to this new life. I promise I will never forget you or stop loving you."

Sam said, "Never in my life have I gotten so close to people. I treasure you, Tab, Cynthia, and Carrie." I told Sam he was precious to me.

My second-to-last night, Tab, Carrie, and I went out together. It was wonderful being with my two friends. We were joyful. Carrie was lively, looking fresh and beautiful. She ate something good and didn't order her usual salad. Tab ordered the most fattening thing on the menu.

When we got back my dad called. "I'm scared, Dad. Now it's up to me to continue to overcome my past."

"You can do it, Cyndi," my confident dad said. "Mom and I will be here, and new friends. We love you very much."

But when I hung up the phone I could feel the old loneliness forming. "No, no, no!" I ran to Carrie and Tab. "I'm afraid. Please help me. I don't want to be afraid." I shared my feelings with the two who loved me, and the fear crumbled. I felt good about my new ability to let my friends know what I needed and to share the feelings I formerly suppressed and then binged to compensate.

Just one more night and I will never sleep here again. God, together we can do it. I'm scared, but you'll be constant; you'll never leave me. Please help me.

Mike and I had our last afternoon together in our therapy room. I was so grateful I did not want to say good-bye. But he said, "Well, how do you want to say good-bye?"

"I want to do it so I will have the least pain."

Mike spoke kindly, saying the little girl's journey was over, that life was waiting for me, and it was up to me to reach out for it. He told me to love people and God, to accept their love, to take care of my body, and nourish my soul. He said, "I don't know what Christ would say to you if you were to see him in person right now; but you picture him sitting here, and listen to what he would say."

I did picture my Lord. He was saying, "Be at peace, Cynthia. I'm here with you. I have always been here. Be patient. I love you. The past is gone and the future will be fulfilling because I will be with you, always."

Then Mike said, giggling, "Picture me riding into town on a giant gorilla when you want to remember me."

My tears fell, but I opened my eyes and sobbed, "Mike, I want to say that you saved my life, helped me save my own life, and I will forever be grateful to you. I will pray for you every day. God has given you a special gift. I am so lucky to have had you find out about my little girl. I want to make you proud of me by being the woman I was made to be." Then I laughed, "And Mike, you're not really fat. I've decided you are just paunchy."

Mike laughed, "Paunchy, huh? Boy, I'll have to tell my wife that one. Paunchy."

"Mike, you are beautiful to me because of who you are. Thank you for saving my life."

Mike patted me on the back and then, in his usual blunt manner, rose quickly and opened the door. As he walked down the hall to the locked door of the psychiatric ward, I yelled, "Hey, Mike Moore, pat yourself on the back and say, 'Yes, world, once again, I, Mike Moore, the magnificent, saved another life.'" Mike laughed and the locked door came between us. "Mike Moore, I love you," I whispered.

A couple hours later, Ryun came. He looked different from the last time I'd seen him. We went for a walk and sat by the creek. "Ryun, let's talk. I know you're afraid of pain, but that's part of life, and part of life is having to say good-bye. Tell me, did you treat me badly last weekend and smoke grass because you were afraid of my leaving?"

"I guess so. When you came into the store and told me that I was hurting and all, I was mad and thought, 'What right do you have, Cynthia, to tell me how I feel?' Then I got to thinking about it and decided you were right."

"Ryun, I love being your friend, and hate to leave you, but I will be in this world if you need me, and there are other friends in your school and church. You have so much to give to people. Give it."

Carrie, Tab, and I stayed up as late as we could, talking and giggling. We had much hope for each other. Both of them had more weight to gain, but we all knew we were going to make it.

My sleep was peaceful. The next day I would say good-bye to my family at the Richardson Medical Center. I also knew my life would never be the same.

My last group session was painful but fulfilling. I asked everyone in the group to tell me what I meant to them, and to be honest. "I need to know how you feel about me, so that when I get down or lonely, I can remember your love."

"You're going to make it, girl. You have much love to give," said one.

Carrie said, "Cynthia, you have given me the will to keep going. You lifted me up, and were a source of comfort. I love you and will never forget you."

Tab said, "Cynthia, you're the sister I never had. You were my strength when I couldn't go on. You have it all, and I love you."

Rachel said, "I'm proud of you. Among all the patients I have encountered, I have yet to see one fight so hard for her life. You are a beautiful person, and don't forget it."

Others said, "I respect you. You shoot from the hip and I appreciate that. I know you care, even though you got disgusted with me at times. I appreciate your total honesty. Write that book. You have the heart to reach a lot of people."

"Well," I said, "it's my turn to tell you how I feel. Tab, you are precious and special to me. Don't live for your dad, live for yourself and for God. I love you."

"Carrie, keep that beautiful head up. Fight for your rights. You deserve to be happy. I love you."

And so I went around the circle. I had no more tears, only smiles. In my heart this hospital family, and the members of the family who had already left, would always be with me.

While I packed my bags, everyone was in my room, talking and giving me little mementos. Tab came in with a big poster that said, "I'm a People Binger." Everyone on the ward had signed it. "I couldn't have asked for a better gift. This will be on my wall forever. Yeah," I looked at everyone crowding into my room, "that's me. I'm a people binger."

The nurse who had taken me up to the ward the first night

hugged me and said, "Don't forget that first night, Cynthia, and thank God for how far you have come."

Good-bye, day room, group, staff, hallway. Good-bye, locked doors.

Tab, Carrie, and I walked to my car and embraced. "Remember, Cynthia, strength can be a weakness. You are beautiful on the inside, and don't forget it! Remember to binge on people."

Both of them kept giving me last-minute advice and encouragement. They promised to fight and not give up themselves.

I drove away and looked at the hospital, the place where I had unlocked my soul and released my monster. I smiled and said, "Good-bye, cocoon. Hello, world!"

My spirit soared, the little girl was smiling, the woman Cynthia was free, free!

Hello, world! Meet Cynthia!

Epilogue

I am sitting on a beach near Portland, Oregon. The little girl had to fill in some gaps on her journey to becoming Cynthia, the woman. Since Portland is where it all began, I came here to rest and find answers to my questions.

First, I tried to find the doctor who treated me for my burns when I was four years old. I learned he died twelve years ago, the same year I became bulimic. My medical records no longer exist, as so many years have gone by.

Next, I went to the house where the little girl grew up. I went to the bedroom where many a night I shook in fear of the monsters outside. I went to the window and looked through the curtains; the monsters, of course, were only trees. The hallway that was long and scary when I was little is really very short. I could hear Mike saying, "Perception, Cynthia!" I entered the room where Robby accidentally pushed me against the vaporizer. I saw the little girl screaming and running, but I, the woman, said to myself, "I am no longer damaged freight."

There was the room where the lonely little girl pretended to be a school teacher or an actress in front of an audience. I saw her sitting on the couch alone, eating her candy bars. I realized this was where it all began, where I found comfort and developed my facade.

I left the house and closed the door. The past is gone, the ghosts are gone, the monsters have been conquered. Good-bye, little girl. The future waits for Cynthia.

I sought out people who had known the little girl, and was told stories I'd never heard before. Most confirmed that Dad seldom talked about me when I was growing up; usually he talked about Robby. That still stung. But now I am an adult he knows me well enough so he can be proud of me.

One old family friend remembered many a Thursday when Dad, having heard of someone in San Francisco who might give some money to the college that he was struggling to keep open, would drive down there. He would sleep in his car because he couldn't afford a motel room. The next day he would get ready for his appointment by washing and shaving in a gas station sink. Maybe the wealthy person would donate a hundred dollars, maybe nothing. After the meeting Dad would drive back to Portland, arrive in the early hours of Sunday morning and catch some sleep. Then we would all get up and drive an hour or more to a church where he preached. That was my dad? Now I understand that he, too, had his share of sorrows and loneliness, but he never told me. Why didn't he tell me? I guess he didn't want to bother me.

I also heard something about my mother that I will never forget. I was burned around Thanksgiving Day. A family asked Mom and Dad to come for dinner, but Mom didn't want to be away from the hospital. However, she did go home for a short time on Thanksgiving Day to cook dinner. The only thing she had in the freezer was liver! For Thanksgiving dinner Robby, Mom, and Dad ate liver, because of me. She never told me that. Why? I guess she didn't want to bother me.

I also came here to see my brother. I explained that one of the reasons I became an over-the-counter drug addict was for him, to prove to him that his little sister wasn't the goody-goody he thought she was. I told him I was never again going to live my life for my family to the detriment of my health.

Now, as I sit on this beach, I see the glorious sight of God's world. The waves roll and my ears are acute to their sounds. The wind feels wonderful on my skin. The sun shines in my face, and my hands touch and grasp the sand around me. I'm alive, I feel! My tears flow freely—happy, rejoicing tears.

God, you are alive and you do love me. Thank you for opening my blind eyes and healing my deaf ears. Thank you, Lord, for my new life. I cherish this life and all the moments you give me.

I am free!

Two weeks after returning home to Oklahoma City from Oregon, I told my story to reporters. It hit the front page of the Sunday Daily Oklahoman. My phone nearly rang off the hook. Within two weeks God enabled me to help over 100 women and families. I asked him to guide me in my new career of sharing my story in person and writing this book in order to help other women who are dying from bulimia and anorexia.

I resigned from the TV station and started making speeches in Arkansas and Texas. In the three months following my hospitalization, I talked to over 300 desperate people, and where I spoke formed support groups for bulimics. I have also discussed communication between teens and their parents.

My life is dedicated to reaching out and telling those who live with the monster, bulimia, that there is hope. I am trying to raise, through the foundation I head, $500,000 to help those without medical insurance to get treatment. Since my work began, scores of women have gone to the Minirth-Meier Clinic in Dallas and been treated for bulimia, anorexia, or other disorders such as depression, either as inpatients or outpatients.

The things I learned from the psychiatrists and psychologists at the clinic have kept me bulimia-free for over a year, and I know I will never regress, because my root problems, stemming from my childhood, were resolved.

Treating Bulimia

Medical and Psychological Perspectives

What is bulimia?

The word *bulimia*, strictly speaking, refers to an insatiable, voracious appetite resulting in excessive eating. But not until 1980 was it formally recognized as a psychiatric diagnosis, when the *Diagnostic and Statistical Manual of Mental Disorders* listed as the criteria for identifying bulimia the following symptoms:[1]

1. Recurrent episodes of binge eating (rapid consumption of a large amount of food in a discrete period of time, usually less than two hours).
2. At least three of the following:
   a. consumption of high-caloric, easily ingested food during a binge.
   b. inconspicuous eating during a binge.

1. The American Psychiatric Association, Quick Reference to the Diagnostic Criteria from DSM-III, 1980, p.44.

    c. termination of such eating episodes by abdominal pain, sleep, social interruption, or self-induced vomiting.

    d. repeated attempts to lose weight by severely restrictive diets, self-induced vomiting, or use of cathartics and/or diuretics.

    e. frequent weight fluctuations greater than ten pounds due to alternating binges and fasts.

3. Awareness that the eating pattern is abnormal and fear of not being able to stop eating voluntarily.

4. Depressed mood and self-deprecating thoughts following eating binges.

5. The bulimic episodes are not due to anorexia nervosa or any known physical disorder.

It is important to notice that bulimia is a psychiatric eating disorder that is different from the overeating or heavy snacking normal people do occasionally and overweight persons may do habitually. It is a disease marked by compulsive, uncontrollable binging and purging, accompanied by depression and, in many instances, other psychological disorders.

During a binge a person ingests huge amounts of food in a short period of time. One can't seem to get food quickly enough before and during a binge, typically eating high-caloric, carbohydrate-rich foods that need little preparation. Bingers eat far beyond the body's normal signals to stop eating. A binge may last from a few minutes to several hours, averaging one to two hours, in which 3,000 calories are consumed. Binges occur from once a week to several times daily.

Only a very small number of bingers are known not to purge, and thereby become obese. Most discover ways to get rid of their food and excess weight by inducing vomiting and taking laxatives or diuretics, which in turn become part of the disease. Obviously, bulimia presents serious threats to one's health, and ultimately to life itself. A few health problems from a much longer list are electrolyte imbalance (which may lead to heart failure), alkalosis, metabolic problems, hormonal abnormalities (including cessation of menstruation), malnutrition, dehydration, and malfunction of many other body functions.

Bulimia and anorexia nervosa

While bulimia and anorexia nervosa—self-induced starvation—are defined and treated as two distinct disorders, both are present in many persons. A fair number of patients are seen who alternate between periods of anorexia nervosa and bulimia; others have them simultaneously.

Persons with the two disorders have several things in common: particularly an obsession with food and calories, and a morbid fear of gaining weight. Therefore, both types may use vomiting, laxatives, and diet pills, plus excessive jogging and exercise.

How many people have bulimia?

Bulimia has been until recently a "closet" disease; sufferers usually successfully hide it from friends, relatives, and spouses for a long time. That, along with the fact that it has been so recently recognized by the scientific community, means that very little research and knowledge of it exists, including accurate counts of sufferers. Present estimates range in the millions in the United States, and everyone who is knowledgeable agrees bulimia is reaching epidemic proportions.

Many more people have bulimia than anorexia nervosa. But anorexia is better known because it is more visible; extremely low body weight cannot be hidden. Also, there has been recent media coverage of well-known personalities with anorexia nervosa. In addition, almost all studies and research of eating disorders up to now have been on anorexia nervosa.

What causes bulimia?

Theories abound as to the causes of bulimia, but as yet no single one has been conclusively proven: However, at our clinic we have, based on our observations of numerous patients, found four general factors which contribute to most mental disorders, of which three are usually significant in bulimia and which form the basis for treatment. These are conflicts, current stress, and the choices we make. We find the weight of the causes to fall on the emotional areas, and it is through addressing them in a multi-disciplinary approach that we have successfully treated bulimia and anorexia nervosa.

What type person gets bulimia?

Bulimia crosses ethnic and socio-economic lines, but our inpatients have been white females between ages 17 and 36, mostly from middle and upper middle-class families. Very few males are known to have bulimia; therefore, it is identified as a disease of young women. Age of onset is generally between the middle teens and early twenties.

These young women appear to be emotionally healthy in most respects, but the scant research that has measured personality traits of anorexic and bulimic patients shows that they tend to be depressed, perfectionists, overly compliant, overly conforming and have low self-esteem.

The bulimic patients tend to fall within normal limits on the test. However, they do display more significant psychopathology than the anorexic patients. Those with bulimia try to deny the existence of any psychological problems and are defensive about revealing their personalities. Further, they seem to be fighting against something, or are indirectly hostile or rebellious. They are dissatisfied with life or with themselves, but do not see this as depression. They are especially punctual and conscientious. They tend to be traditionally feminine in their interests, domestic activities and career choices, and may be passive in their roles. Finally, tension, depression, anxiety, obsessions, and guilt characterize the eating disorder patients.

These patients have a tendency to be very sensitive to society's emphasis on slimness, good looks, and popularity. We also see ambivalence regarding their sexual identities and roles. They strive for good grades in school and excellent performance in the arts. There are, of course, individual exceptions to all of the above.

What about the families of bulimic patients?

As we have said, unresolved childhood conflicts are major factors in the eating disorders; therefore, family dynamics make a crucial contribution to the causes and cure of bulimia.

Generally, our patients come from good homes with good parents who have made a few accidental errors in raising their children. The fathers are intelligent, hard working, financially and professionally successful, and highly regarded for their contributions to society and their concerns for other people. These men often inadvertently overlook the needs of their own children, leaving childrearing to the mothers.

Fathers of many of our patients are strict, logical, and show little emotion. Their daughters strive to appear and perform well in a bid for the attention and affection they do not receive from their fathers, and in turn to receive attention from other males who are father substitutes.

We find the mothers to be generally responsible, conscientious and loving parents, but who may be overwhelmed by and somewhat resentful of the pressures of being in charge of the household and rearing their children largely by themselves. They, too, crave their husband's and children's attention, and outside recognition as well. Some mothers, in their competition for attention, subconsciously alienate their husbands and children from each other. Many are attractive women and openly concerned with their weight and dieting, although they freely dispense food to their children as an act of love.

The daughters of such families, then, receive mixed signals and draw mixed conclusions about themselves: self-worth is based on appearance and performance; being "sexy" draws male attention, about which they then feel guilty; they fear intimacy with males because they were never close to their fathers; they sense their mothers' frustrations with their woman's roles and develop ambivalence regarding their own femininity. Their internal struggles between wanting to be physically attractive to men and wanting to keep them at a distance by being unattractive can keep such women in the anorexia-bulimia cycle, while food becomes the substitute for love when they are lonely.

We emphasize again that these are general patterns we have observed, and that there are many individual exceptions.

How is bulimia treated?

Immediate hospitalization is often necessary because patients come to us in a medical crisis or are suicidal. Treatment of these conditions takes priority on admission. Physical examinations, laboratory tests, EEGs and CAT scans are administered, medical specialists may be consulted, vital signs are brought back to normal as quickly as possible, and the patients are immediately placed on individually planned, balanced, nutritious diets. The average length of stay is six weeks; Cynthia stayed ten. Further outpatient treatment of up to two years benefits most patients.

The hospital provides the patient a milieu or environment of total control that removes her from stressful situations; allows her the time and provides a safe place to face her worst fears and deepest pains as she concentrates on self-exploration through intense therapy; and makes available a nursing staff around the clock, plus a group of other patients, for emotional support and socializing.

A therapy team works on initial and ongoing evaluation of and involvement in the patient's therapy program. Team members include a psychiatrist, psychologist, therapist, dietician, occupational therapist, and the nursing staff. The patient, too, takes part in her evaluation, in setting goals for her improvement, and in understanding the purpose of her therapy. Her food intake is measured and she is closely watched to prevent vomiting after meals.

Because of the complexity of both bulimia and anorexia nervosa, with many factors contributing to the diseases, therapy is multidisciplinary, utilizing the findings and experiences of our own clinic personnel and those of others in medicine and psychiatry. This multifaceted program consists of the following: behavior modification (rewards, such as passes and visitors, for reaching goals); daily journal written by the patient (Cynthia's story is based on her journal); daily monitor sheet kept by the patient, recording her times of urges to binge and purge, and clues as to what she experiences at those times (helpful in providing the therapy team and patient with patterns of behavior and vulnerability); occupational therapy; and psychotherapy, consisting of individual therapy, group therapy, and family therapy.

Individual and group therapy sessions are intense and active experiences, in which the therapist demonstrates an emotional involvement with the patient's problem, and evokes an emotional response as she uncovers and relives traumatic past events and unresolved emotional conflicts. The patient's insights are used to guide her in outgrowing her emotional alienation and chronic childhood roles, correcting her attitudes and behaviors, strengthening her self-trust, improving her interpersonal relationships, and depending on multiple resources in seeking emotional nurture. In other words, it is through psychotherapy that the compulsively self-destroying monster is exposed and banished.

Medication is necessary for many patients. Antidepressants correct the biochemically based depression that often accompanies and seems to be related to bulimia, a depression that has symptoms of suicidal thoughts, fatigue, disturbed sleep, and a deep sense of guilt or worthlessness. In many cases this medication controls the binge-purge cycle. Antidepressants are not the same as sedatives or tranquilizers that may merely cover up symptoms. Antidepressants are nonaddictive, producing no tolerance and no withdrawal. The most often used antidepressants are imapramine and MAO inhibitors.

Our goal in treating women with bulimia is to move them toward the realization that they are able to make choices, responsible choices that will aid their recovery. We all make wrong choices; we all sin at times; but we can admit this and make new choices. This is especially true of Christians, for we can overcome our problems. Therefore, a source of encouragement for the staff and patients is found in Philippians 4:13: "I can do all things through him who strengthens me."

Knowing and growing in Christ makes the bulimic person realize she does not have to prove her worth to him. She does not have to be or do anything to gain his love and acceptance. Salvation is free, and all she needs to do is accept that.

Paul Meier, M.D.
Frank Minirth, M.D.
Luis Gutierrez, M.D.
Michael Moore, M.S., M.Div.
Richard Flournoy, Ph.D.

We would like to express our thanks to the nursing staff of the Psychiatry Unit at Richardson Medical Center, especially Carol Williams, R.N., and to Maj-Britt Morgan, R.N., the head nurse at Memorial Hospital of Garland, for their help, understanding, support, and contributions in the treatment of eating disorders.

12 Years Later
and Counting

Marion is fifteen. She is going to die unless she starts eating. She eats only one apple a day while continuing to function in school, maintaining a 4.0 grade average so she can get into a preppy college.

Courtney was twenty-two years old when bulimia gripped her life. Engaged to be married, she was suddenly seized by fear. She was afraid if she didn't have the "perfect" body, her fiancé would reject her.

Sunny looked at me and said, "I feel like I'm drowning." I had just finished telling my story and had asked the audience to express feelings.

Lisa was only sixteen. Beautiful, popular, a cheerleader everyone loved, she secretly struggled with bulimia. Outside she looked like she had it altogether. Inside she was dying. One Tuesday she had breakfast with friends, went to school, left for home at lunch time, went into her room, closed the door, and died four hours later from an overdose of painkillers.

Heather fought hard against bulimia and suicidal thoughts. After therapy she married a wonderful guy and they had a child. But her laxative addiction while she was bulimic took its toll. Half her intestine was recently removed and she now wears a colon bag.

I wish I could say that eating disorders have declined since this book was first published in 1984. But judging from the letters I receive each week, the people who approach me at my lectures, or ask me personally to help them, I know that bulimia, anorexia, and compulsive overeating are on the rise. It seems body obsession is starting younger. At one time sixteen-year-olds were into binge eating. Now I meet twelve-year-olds near death from bulimia and anorexia. The statistic that one out of three college coeds have an eating disorder has not changed.

Why all this emphasis on having the perfect body? The media may have some influence in making the "waif" look popular, but I believe the real answer is that an eating disorder is a red-light signal that something is seriously wrong with the "heart."

This signal often points to family and past hurts, such as, abandonment or neglect, abuse (sexual, physical, emotional, verbal, spiritual), trauma (a death, accident, intentional pain, divorce, separation, rape), rejection, high expectations from parents, lack of nurturing.

A major factor in counseling an individual with an eating disorder is to try to understand what the eating disorder is accomplishing for her. A basic clue in uncovering the answer may be to determine when the disorder began. Usually the eating disorder was triggered as a numbing behavior. What starts as a behavior can quickly become an addiction.

Take a closer look at fifteen-year-old Marion.

"When did you stop eating?" I ask Marion.

"When I was thirteen," she answers.

"Any specific hurts or traumas at that time?" I probe. She can't identify any.

When I talked to her family, I learned that she was sexually molested at age four by a step-brother. Courageous four-year-old Marion told her family. The family took action, the court got involved, and the step-brother was forced into therapy for five years. The four-year-old saw a therapist too. The step-brother and family told Marion how sorry they were (a remarkable step) and life went on.

Marion reaches puberty. Her body changes to that of a young woman. Her breasts develop and her period begins. Teenager Marion is scared. Boys might like her. Without really knowing why, she stops eating. No food means that Marion stays "safely" a little girl and no guy will be attracted to a child.

When Marion ate, flashbacks of her sexual abuse came alive. Starving numbed her, masked her history of sexual trauma, her flashbacks shut off, and she didn't remember the pain.

Marion needs to remember so she can heal and forgive. She needs to find a safe place, a safe person, so she can relive the past, confront the shame, get angry, relive even more memories, get angry some more, and with time, ultimately forgive.

Courtney has a more complicated history. She had never bonded with her dad who was engrossed in creating a business. He showed Courtney no emotion and was highly critical of both mother and daughter. He ignored his wife's talents and appearance. That mindset triggered Courtney's deep feelings of inadequacy, feelings that were compounded because her mother rarely was tender and loving toward her.

At age thirteen she was raped by a "friend." She told no one because she thought it was her fault. At age sixteen she had a relationship with an abusive man in his late twenties. At age eighteen, in another abusive relationship, Courtney became pregnant. Her embarrassed parents sent her away. Alone, desperate, she yielded to the boyfriend's plea to get married. The disastrous marriage ended soon in divorce after which she and her baby moved back in with her parents.

Courtney finished college and met a wonderful man. He loved her and her child. They married. So why was she excessively exercising, binging, and purging? Why wasn't she free to enjoy her happiness? Her eating disorder numbed her need to deal with the unresolved conflicts of the past.

I watch as Courtney step by step goes to her past and deals with the feelings she stuffed for so long. She is determined to leave the past behind and go on with her new life.

People with eating disorders always harbor intense inner pain or locked-up secrets. Often they don't realize the depth of their pain because of the numbing effects of their eating disorder. For ten years now I've told thousands the story of how I kept my bulimia secret for twelve years, how I nearly died, and how I finally found the answers and overcame.

Through my story, readers can experience their own locked-up hurts, abandonment, and abuse. They can relive their past and see where mom and dad made serious mistakes, and can come to understand those actions as sometimes intentional but often unintentional in nature or done out of ignorance. It is easy to see how the dysfunctional cycle can continue through their own actions.

For a person with an eating disorder to get well, she has to be sick of being sick. She must find a professional or someone who knows how to deal with the past. Bulimia is almost impossible to overcome if therapy is only behavioral: eat slowly, eat three meals a day, drink water if you are unhappy.

For me, having my parents come into my therapy and deal with my upbringing was essential for healing. Only if parents, siblings, or mates have the ability to look at themselves and the family relationships honestly and empathetically, should they be involved in the therapy. They need to be willing to self-disclose their roles in the eating disorder. Family members need to give each other permission to reveal their hearts and the right to confront and disclose past hurts.

Whatever the abuse issues, the family must be open to hear the bulimic's pain. They must be willing to acknowledge the pain and understand their personal role in its cause. People have addictions for a reason. Too often the reason resides in the family. Bulimia is a family problem.

If a family is too dysfunctional to acknowledge problems or unwilling to participate in therapy, the bulimic needs to find friends who can become surrogate families, offering empathy, understanding, and support.

Healing can and does come when parents do all they can to make sure their child, of whatever age, gets help.

Treatment for an eating disorder can be brief to extensive. The duration, frequency, intensity, and purpose is different for different people. Going to an eating disorder clinic or hospital can be of immense help. Often clinics are expensive and only rarely will insurance companies cover the cost. My hope for the future is for residential homes to be set up for those who suffer eating disorders. This would keep room and board costs to a minimum while still maintaining therapy and good care.

If you can't go to a hospital, find a therapist, support group, pastor, or friends to help you. My therapist and I now do intensive "Hope for the Hungry Heart Weeks" for those I call "functional bulimics." They can work and function and do not need hospitalization but do require intensive work. Those intensive weeks, offered periodically, provide a safe environment where eating disorder sufferers can confront their pain and receive love, support, and hope.

In the past year three beautiful women I have known died because of their eating disorders. I don't want to lose another precious life. That is why I'm driven to speak about my story. I believe there are reasons why you or someone you love has an eating disorder.

I believe in facing truth because as Jesus said, "Know the truth and the truth will set you free." So I ask you, "What is your truth?" I encourage you to ask yourself that question. Embrace the answers. Face the pain, Grieve. Get angry and grieve some more. Confront. With time and grace, ultimately forgive the people who hurt you and abandoned you and abused you. Then forgive yourself.

It's been twelve years now and I can say to you, "I am no longer bulimic." I celebrate the person God intended me to be. I still am striving to be "The King's daughter." My life after addiction has been an incredible journey—not perfect or without heartache. Two years after I wrote *The Monster Within,* I was diagnosed with breast cancer and had a modified radical masectomy and chemotherapy. But I fought for my life because life was worth fighting for.

Ten years later I'm married to a precious man and I have two beautiful sons. I have a full-time profession speaking to various groups and see lives being touched because of my painful journey. Yes, life goes on after bulimia. Believe it.

If you feel hopeless today, I give you my hope.
If you need courage, I give you my courage.
I encourage you from my heart.
Never give up.
Don't let those who hurt you, left you, abandoned you, win.
Get well, life is waiting for you.

Cynthia Rowland McClure

More information about books Cynthia has written on eating disorders, her speaking schedule, or Hope for the Hungry Heart weeks is available from:

Hope for the Hungry Heart
8A Village Loop Road, Suite 140
Pomona, CA 91766 (909) 628-8732